WILL SHAKESPEARE

AN INVENTION IN FOUR ACTS

BY

CLEMENCE DANE

New York

THE MACMILLAN COMPANY

1936

Press of
J. J. Little & Ives Company
New York, U. S. A.

'There's a divinity that shapes our ends,
Rough-hew them how we will.'

SHAKESPEARE.

THE PEOPLE OF THE PLAY

As they appear.

Anne Hathaway.
Will Shakespeare.
Mrs. Hathaway.
Henslowe.
A Child.
Players.
Queen Elizabeth.
Mary Fitton.
Kit Marlowe.
Stage Hands.
A Boy.
A Landlord.
A Man.
Another Man.
A Girl.
A Street Hawker.
A Page.
Soldiers, Attendants, etc.

ACT I.—A Cottage in Stratford.

ACT II.—Ten Years Later—*Scene* 1. A Room in the Palace. *Scene* 2. Three Months Later—The First Night of "Romeo and Juliet."

ACT III.—*Scene* 1. A Month Later—Shakespeare's Lodging. *Scene* 2. The Same Night—A Room at an Inn.

ACT IV.—The Next Day—A State Room in the Palace.

The Play was first acted at the Shaftesbury Theatre, London, on November 17th, 1921, by the Reandean Company, with the following cast:—

WILL SHAKESPEARE	Mr. Philip Merivale
ANNE	Miss Moyna Macgill
MRS. HATHAWAY	Miss Mary Rorke
HENSLOWE	Mr. Arthur Whitby
QUEEN ELIZABETH	Miss Haidee Wright
MARY FITTON	Miss Mary Clare
KIT MARLOWE	Mr. Claude Rains
A CHILD ACTOR	Master Eric Spear
A SECRETARY	Mr. Arthur Bawtree
A STAGE HAND	Mr. Gilbert Ritchie
A BOY	Master Spear
A LANDLORD	Mr. Ivor Barnard
A LADY-IN-WAITING	Miss Joan Maclean

Shadows in Act I.

OPHELIA	Miss Lennie Pride	SHYLOCK	Mr. Gilbert Ritchie
DESDEMONA	Miss Gladys Jessel	CLOWN	Mr. Ivor Barnard
OTHELLO	Mr. Herbert Young	HAMLET	Mr. Neil Curtis
QUEEN MARGARET	Miss Flora Robson	CAESAR	Mr. Arthur Bawtree
PRINCE ARTHUR	Mr. Eric Crosbie	CLEOPATRA	Miss Mai Ashley
ROSALIND	Miss Phyllis Fabian	KING LEAR	Mr. Fred Morgan

THE THREE FATES { Miss Nora Robinson
Miss Gladys Gray
Miss Beatrice Smith

Strolling Players, Beefeaters, Stage Hands, Drinkers, Court Attendants, etc.

The Production by BASIL DEAN.
The Music by THOMAS WOOD.
Designs for the Scenery and Dresses by GEORGE HARRIS.

ACT I.

*The curtain rises on the living room of a sixteenth century cottage.
The walls and ceiling are of black beams and white-washed
plaster. On the left is a large oven fireplace with logs burning.
Beyond it is a door. At the back is another door and a
mullioned window half open giving a glimpse of bare garden
hedge and winter sky. On the right wall is a staircase running
down from the ceiling into the room, a dresser and a light shelf
holding a book or two. Under the shelf is a small table piled
with papers, ink-stand, sand box and so on. At it sits* SHAKE-
SPEARE, *his elbows on his papers, his head in his hands, absorbed.
He is a boy of twenty but looks older. He is dark and slight.
His voice is low, but he speaks very clearly. Behind him* ANNE
HATHAWAY *moves to and fro from dresser to the central table,
laying a meal. She is a slender, pale woman with reddish hair.
Her movements are quick and furtive and she has a high sweet
voice that shrills too easily.*

ANNE [*hesitating, with little pauses between the sentences*].

> Supper is ready, Will! Will, did you hear?
> A farm-bird—Mother brought it. Won't you
> come?
> She's crying in for the basket presently.
> First primroses! Here, smell! Sweet, aren't they?
> Bread?
> Are the snow wreaths gone from the fields? Did
> you go far?
> Are you wet? Was it cold? There's black frost
> in the air,

My mother says, and spring hangs dead on the
   boughs—
Oh, you might answer when I speak to you!

   SHAKESPEARE *gets up quickly.*

Where are you going?

SHAKESPEARE.   Out!
ANNE.   Where?
SHAKESPEARE.   Anywhere—
ANNE. —away from me! Yes! Say it!
SHAKESPEARE. [*under his breath*].   Patience! Patience!
ANNE. Come back! Come back! I'm sorry. Oh, come
   back!
I talk too much. I crossed you. You must eat.
Oh! Oh! I meant no harm—I meant no harm!—
You know?

SHAKESPEARE.   I know.
ANNE.   Why, then, come back and eat,
And talk to me. Aren't you a boy to lose
All day in the woods?

SHAKESPEARE.   The town!
ANNE.   Ah! In the town?
Ah, then, you've talked and eaten. Yes, you can
   talk
In the town!

   He goes back to his desk.
                    More writing? What's the dream
                    to-day?

   He winces.

Oh, tell me, tell me!

SHAKESPEARE.   No!
ANNE.   I want your dreams

SHAKESPEARE. A dream's a bubble, Anne, and yet a world,
Unsailed, uncharted, mine. But stretch your hand
To touch it—gone! And you have wet your fingers,
Whilst I, like Alexander, want my world—
And so I scold my wife.

ANNE.   Oh, let me sail
Your world with you.

SHAKESPEARE.   One day, when all is mapped
On paper—

ANNE.   Now!

SHAKESPEARE.   Not yet.

ANNE.   Now, now!

SHAKESPEARE.   I cannot!

ANNE. Because you will not. Ever you shut me out.

SHAKESPEARE. How many are there in the listening room ?

ANNE. We two.

SHAKESPEARE.   We three.

ANNE.   Will!

SHAKESPEARE.   Are there not three? Yet swift,
Because it is too soon, you shrink from me,
Guarding your mystery still; so must I guard
My dreams from any touch till they are born.

ANNE. What! Do you make our bond our barrier now?

SHAKESPEARE. See, you're a child that clamours—"Let me taste!"
But laugh and let it sip your wine, it cries—
"I like it not. It is not sweet!"—and blames you.
See! even when I give you cannot take.

ANNE. Try me!

SHAKESPEARE.   Too late.

ANNE.   I will not think I know
What cruelty you mean. What is't you mean?
What is't?

SHAKESPEARE.   How long since we two married?
ANNE.   Why,
Four months.
SHAKESPEARE.   And are you happy?
ANNE.   Will, aren't you?
SHAKESPEARE. I asked my wife.
ANNE.   I am! I am! I am!
Oh, how can I be happy when I read
Your eyes, and read—what is it that I read?
SHAKESPEARE. God knows!
ANNE. Yes, God He knows, but He's so far away—
Tell Anne!
SHAKESPEARE. Touch not these cellar thoughts, half worm, half
            weed:
Give them no light, no air: be warned in time:
Break not the seal nor roll away the stone,
Lest the blind evil writhe itself heart-high
And its breath stale us!
ANNE.   Oh, what evil?
SHAKESPEARE.   Know you not?
Why then I'll say "Thank God!" and never tell
            you—
And yet I think you know?
ANNE.   Am I, your wife,
Wiser than your own mother in your ways
(For she was wise for many, I've but you)
Ways in my heart stored, and with them the unborn
I feed, that he may grow a second you—
Am I your wife, so close to you all day,
So close to you all night, that oft I lie
Counting your heart-beats—do I watch you stir
And cry out suddenly and clench your hand

Till the bone shows white, and then you sigh and
    turn,
And sometimes smile, but never ope your eyes,
Nor know me with a seeking touch of hands
That bids me share the dream—am I your wife,
Can I be woman and your very wife
And know not you are burdened? You lock me out,
Yet at the door I wait, wringing my hands
To help you.

SHAKESPEARE.   You could help me; but—I know you!
You'd help me, in your way, to go—your way!

ANNE.   The right way.

SHAKESPEARE.   Said I not, sweetheart—your way?
So—leave it!

    He begins to write. ANNE *goes to the window
    and leans against it looking out.*

ANNE [*softly*].   Give me words! God, give me words!

SHAKESPEARE. Sweetheart, you stay the light.

ANNE.   The pane is cool.

    She moves to one side.

Can you see now?

SHAKESPEARE.   That's better.

    The twang of a lute is heard.

ANNE.   The road dances.

A VOICE [*singing*].   Come with me to London,
        Folly, come away!
    I'll make your fortune
        On a fine day—

ANNE.   A stranger with my mother at the gate!

    She opens the door to MRS. HATHAWAY, *who
    enters.*

THE VOICE [*nearer*].　　　Daisy leave and buttercup!
　　　　　　　　　　　　Pick your gold and silver up,
　　　　　　　　　　　　　　In London, in London,
　　　　　　　　　　　　　　　Oh, London Town!

ANNE.　　　　What have you brought us, Mother, unawares?

MRS. HATHAWAY.　Why, I met the man in the lane and he asked his way here. He wants Will.

ANNE.　Does he, and does he?

SHAKESPEARE [*at the window*].
　　　　　　　　　One of the players. In the town I met him
　　　　　　　　　And had some talk, and told him of my play.

ANNE.　　　　You told a stranger and a player? But I—
　　　　　　　　　I am not told!

THE VOICE [*close at hand*].
　　　　　　　　　　　For sheep can feed
　　　　　　　　　　　And robins breed
　　　　　　　　　　　Without you, without you,
　　　　　　　　　　And the world get on without you—
　　　　　　　　　　　Oh, London Town!

　　　　　　　SHAKESPEARE *goes to the door.*

ANNE [*stopping him*].　　　What brings him here?

SHAKESPEARE.　　　　　　　　　　　I bring him!
　　　　　　　To my own house. [*He goes out.*]

MRS. HATHAWAY.　　　　　　Trouble?

ANNE.　　　　　　　　　　　　Why, no! No trouble!
　　　　　　　I am not beaten, starved, nor put on the street.

MRS. HATHAWAY. Be wise, be wise; for the child's sake, be wiser!

ANNE.　　　　What shall I do? Out of your fifty years,
　　　　　　　What shall I do to hold him?

MRS. HATHAWAY.　　　　　　　　　A low voice
　　　　　　　And a light heart is best—and not to judge.

ANNE. Light, Mother, light? Oh, Mother, Mother, Mother!
I'm battling on the crumble-edge of loss
Against a seaward wind, that drives his ship
To fortunate isles, but carries me cliff over,
Clutching at flint and thistle-hold, to braise me
Upon the barren beaches he has left
For ever.

> SHAKESPEARE *and the player,* HENSLOWE, *come in talking.*

MRS. HATHAWAY [*at the inner door*].
Come, find my basket for me. Let them be!

ANNE. Look at him, how his face lights up!

MRS. HATHAWAY. Come now,
And leave them to it!

ANNE. I dare not, Mother, I dare not.

MRS. HATHAWAY. It's not the way—a little trust—

ANNE. I dare not.

> MRS. HATHAWAY *goes out at the door by the fire.*

HENSLOWE [*in talk. He is a stout, good-humoured, elderly man, with bright eyes and a dancing step. He wears ear-rings, is dressed shabby-handsome, and is splashed with mud. A lute is slung at his shoulder*]. Played? It shall be played. That's why I'm here.

ANNE [*behind them*]. Will!

SHAKESPEARE [*turning*]. This is my wife.

ANNE [*curtseys. Then, half aside*]. Who is the man? Where from? What is his name?

HENSLOWE [*overhearing*]. Proteus, Madonna! A poor son of the god.

> SHAKESPEARE *laughs.*

ANNE. A foreigner?

HENSLOWE. Why, yes and no! I'm from Spain at the moment—I have castles there; but my bed-sitting room (a green room, Madonna) is in Blackfriars. As to my means, for I see your eye on my travel stains, I have a bank account, also in Spain, a box office, and the best of references. The world and his wife employ me, the Queen comes to see me, and all the men of genius run to be my servants. But as to who I am—O Madonna, who am I not? I've played every card in the pack, beginning as the least in the company, the mere unit, the innocent ace, running up my number with each change of hand to Jack, Queen, King, and so to myself again, the same mere One, but grown to my hopes. For Queen may blow kisses, King of Hearts command all hands at court, but Ace in his shirt-sleeves is manager and trumps them off the board at will. You may learn from this Ace; for I think, sir, you will end as he does, the master of your suit.

ANNE. A fortune-teller too!

HENSLOWE. Will you cross my palm with a sixpence, Madonna?

ANNE. With nothing.

HENSLOWE. Beware lest I tell you for nothing that you—fear your fortune!

SHAKESPEARE [*spreading his hand*]. Is mine worth fearing?

HENSLOWE. Here's an actor's hand, and a bad one. You'll lose your words, King o' Hearts. Your great scenes will break down.

SHAKESPEARE. Then I'll be 'prenticed direct to the Ace.

HENSLOWE. Too fast. You must come to cues like the rest of us, and play out your part, before you can be God Almighty in the wings—as God himself found out when the world was youngish.

ANNE. We're plain people, sir, and my husband works his farm.

HENSLOWE. And sings songs? I've been trying out a new play in the provinces before we risk London and Gloriana—

ANNE. What! the Queen! the Queen?

HENSLOWE. Oh, she keeps her eye on poor players as well as on
Burleigh and the fleet. *There's* God Almighty in the wings if you
like ! But as I say—

> Whatever barn we storm, here in the west,
> We're marching to the echo of new songs,
> Jigged out in taverns, trolled along the street,
> Loosed under sweetheart windows, whistled and
>   sighed
> Wherever a farmer's boy in Lover's Lane
> Shifts from the right foot to the left and waits—
> "Where did you hear it?" say I, beating time:
> And always comes the answer—"Stratford
>   way!"

A green parish, Stratford!

SHAKESPEARE. Too flat, though I love it. Give me hills to climb!

HENSLOWE. Flat? You should see Norfolk, where I was a boy.
From sky to sky there's no break in the levels but shock-head willows
and reed tussocks where a singing bird may nest. But in which?
Oh, for that you must sit unstirring in your boat, between still water
and still sky, while the drips run off your blade until, a yard away,
uprises the song. Then, flash! part the rushes—the nest is bare
and the bird your own! Oh, I know the ways of the water birds!
And so, hearing of a cygnet on the banks of Avon—

ANNE. Ah!

HENSLOWE. You're right, Madonna, the poetical vein runs dry.
So I'll end with a plain question—"Is not Thames broader than
Avon?"

SHAKESPEARE. Muddier—

HENSLOWE. But a magical water to hasten the moult, to wash
white a young swan's feathers.

SHAKESPEARE. Or black, Mephisto!

HENSLOWE. Black swans are rarest. I saw one when I was last in London. London's a great city! Madonna, you should send your husband to market in London, and in a twelvemonth he'll bring you home the world in his pocket as it might be a russet apple.

ANNE. What should we do with the world, sir, here in Stratford?

HENSLOWE. Why, seed it and sow it, and plant it in your garden, and it'll grow into the tree of knowledge.

ANNE [*turning away*]. My garden is planted already.

HENSLOWE [*in a low voice*].

          The black swan seeks a mate, black swan.

SHAKESPEARE.   A woman?

ANNE [*turning sharply*]. What did he say to you?

HENSLOWE. Why, that a woman can make her fortune in London as well as a man. There's one came lately to court, but sixteen and a mere knight's daughter, without a penny piece, and you should see her now! The men at her feet—

ANNE. And the women—?

HENSLOWE. Under her heel.

ANNE.   What does the Queen say?

HENSLOWE.   Winks and 'lets her be,
A fashion out of fashion—gipsy-black
Among the ladies with their bracken hair,
(The Queen, you know, is red!)

SHAKESPEARE.   A vixen, eh?

HENSLOWE.   Treason, my son!

ANNE.   God made us anyway and coloured us!

SHAKESPEARE.   And is he less the artist if at will
He strings a black pearl, hangs between the camps
Of day and day the banner of His dark?
Or that He leaves, when with His autumn breath
He fans the bonfire of the woods, a pine
Unkindled?

HENSLOWE.   True; and such a black is she
Among the golden women.

SHAKESPEARE.   I see your pine,
Your branching solitude, your evening tree,
With high, untroubled head, that meets the eye
As lips meet unseen kisses in the night—
A perfumed dusk, a canopy of dreams
And chapel of ease, a harp for summer airs
To tremble in—

ANNE.   Barren the ground beneath,
No flowers, no grass, the needles lying thick,
Spent arrows—

SHAKESPEARE.   Yes, she knows—we know how
                                    women
Can prick a man to death with needle stabs.

ANNE.   O God!
HENSLOWE.   Your wife! She's ill!
SHAKESPEARE.   Anne?
ANNE.   Let me be!
SHAKESPEARE. Come to your mother—take my arm—
ANNE.   I'll sit.
I have no strength.

SHAKESPEARE.   I'll call her to you. [*He goes out.*]
ANNE.   Quick!
Before he comes, what is her name? her name?
Her mood? her mind? In all the town of
    Stratford
Was there no door but this to pound at? Quick!
You know her? Did you see his look? O God!
The last rope parts. He's like a boat that strains,
Strains at her moorings. Why did you praise
    her so?

And talk of London? What's it all to you?
Tall, is she? Yes, like a tree—a block of wood—
You said so! (Is he coming?) Tell me quick!
I've never seen a London lady close.
She's lovely? So are many! How?

HENSLOWE.
                                She's new!
She's gallant, like a tall ship setting sail,
And boasts she fears no man. Say "woman"
    though—

ANNE.   What woman does this woman fear?
HENSLOWE.
                           The Queen.
I've seen it in her eye.

ANNE.   I should not fear.
HENSLOWE.
You never saw the Queen of England smile
And crook her finger, once—and the fate falls.

ANNE.
I've seen her picture. She's eaten of a worm
As I am eaten. I'd not fear the Queen.
Her snake would know its fellow in my heart
And pass me. But this woman—what's her name?

HENSLOWE.   Mary—
ANNE.
         That's "bitter." I shall find her so.
   SHAKESPEARE *comes in with* MRS. HATHAWAY.
Look at him ! Fear the Queen ? Did not the
    Queen,
My sister, meet a Mary long ago
That bruised her in the heel?

HENSLOWE.
                Man, your wife's mad!
She says the Queen's her sister.

ANNE.
               Mad, noble Festus?
Not I ! But tell him so—he'll kiss you for it.

HENSLOWE.   I'll meet you, friend, some other time or place—
SHAKESPEARE.   What's this? You're leaving us?

HENSLOWE.   Your wife's too ill—

SHAKESPEARE.   Too ill to stand, yet not too ill to—[*Aside*] Anne!
Why does he stare? What have you told my
     friend?

ANNE.   Your friend!

SHAKESPEARE.   My friend!

ANNE.   This once-met Londoner!
What does he want of you, in spite of me?
This bribing tramp, this palpable decoy—

SHAKESPEARE.   Be silent in my house before my friends!
Be silent!

ANNE.   This your friend!

SHAKESPEARE.   Silent, I say!

ANNE.   I *will* not! Blows? Would you do that to me,
Husband?

SHAKESPEARE.   I never touched you!

ANNE.   What! No blow?
Here, where I felt it—here? Is there no wound,
No black mark?

MRS. HATHAWAY.   Oh, she's wild! I'll take her.
Come!
Come, Anne! It's naught! I know the signs.
    [*To* SHAKESPEARE].
                   Stay you!

ANNE.   O Mother, there befell me a strange pang
Here at my heart—[*The two go out together.*]

SHAKESPEARE.   O women! women! women!
They slink about you, noiseless as a cat,
With ready smiles and ready silences.
These women are too humble and too wise
In pricking needle-ways: they drive you mad
With fibs and slips and kisses out of time:

And if you do not trip and feign as they
And cover all with kisses, do but wince
Once in your soul (the soul they shall not touch,
Never, I tell you, never! Sooner the smeared,
The old-time honey death from a thousand stings,
Than let their tongue prick patterns on your soul!)
Then, then all's cat-like clamour and annoy!

HENSLOWE.   Cry, "Shoo!" and clap your hands; for so are all
Familiar women. These are but interludes
In the march of the play, and should be taken so,
Lightly, as food for laughter, not for rage.

SHAKESPEARE.   My mother—
HENSLOWE [*shrugging*].   Ah, your mother!
SHAKESPEARE.   She's not thus,
But selfless; and I've dreamed of others—tall,
Warm-flushed like pine-woods with their clear
          red stems,
With massy hair and voices like the wind
Stirring the cool dark silence of the pines.
Know you such women?—beckoning hill-top
          women,
That sway to you with lovely gifts of shade
And slumber, and deep peace, and when at dawn
You go from them on pilgrimage again,
They follow not nor weep, but rooted stand
In their own pride for ever—demi-gods.
Are there such women? Did you say you knew
Such women? such a woman?

HENSLOWE.   Come to London
And use your eyes!

SHAKESPEARE.   How can I come to London?
You see me what I am, a man tied down.

My wife—you saw! How can I come to London?
Say to a sick man "Take your bed and walk!"
Say to a prisoner "Release your chain!"
Say to a tongue-slit blackbird "Pipe again
As in the free, the spring-time!" You maybe
Have spells to help them, but for me no help.
London!
I think sometimes that I shall never see
This lady in whose lap the weed-hung ships
From ocean-end returning pour their gold,
Myrrh, frankincense. What colour's frank-
            incense?
And how will a man's eye move and how his hand,
Who sailed the flat world round and home again
To London, London of the mazy-streets,
Where ever the shifting people flash and fade
Like my own thoughts? You're smiling—why?
                                    I live there.

HENSLOWE.
SHAKESPEARE.   Oh, to be you!
To read the faces and to write the dreams,
To hear the voices and record the songs,
To grave upon the metal of my mind
All great men, lordlier than they know themselves,
And fowler-like to fling my net o'er London,
And some let fly, and clip the wings of some
Fit for my notes; till one fine day I catch
The Governess of England as she goes
To solemn service with her gentlemen:
(What thoughts behind the mask, beneath the
            crown?)
Queen! The crowd's eyes are yours, but not my
            eyes!

Queen! To my piping you shall unawares
Strut on my stage for me! You laugh? I swear
I'll make that thrice-wrapped, politic, vain heart
My horn-book (as you all are) whence I'll learn
How Julius frowned, and Elinor rode her way
Rough-shod, and Egypt met ill-news. I'll do it,
Though I hold horses in the streets for hire,
Once I am come to London.

HENSLOWE.   Come with us
And there's no holding horses! Part and pay
Are ready, and we start to-night.

SHAKESPEARE.   I cannot.
I'm Whittington at cross-roads, but the bells
Ring " Turn again to Stratford ! " not to London.

HENSLOWE.   Well—as you choose!
SHAKESPEARE.   As I choose? *I! I* choose?
I'm married to a woman near her time
That needs me! Choose? I am not twenty, sir!
What devil sped you here to bid me choose?
I knew a boy went wandering in a wood,
Drunken with common dew and beauty-mad
And moonstruck. Then there came a nightshade
    witch,
Locked hands with him, small hands, hot hands,
    down drew him,
Sighing—"Love me, love me!" as a ring-dove
    sighs,
(How white a woman is, under the moon!)
She was scarce human. Yet he took her home,
And now she's turned in the gross light of day
To a haggard scold, and he handfasted sits
Breaking his heart—and yet the spell constrains
    him.

> This is not I, not I, for I am bound
> To a good wife and true, that loves me; but—
> I tell you I could write of such a man,
> And make you laugh and weep at such a man,
> For your own manhood's sake, so bound, so bound.

HENSLOWE. Laugh? Weep? No, I'd be a friend to such a man! Go to him now and tell him from me—or no! Go rather to this wife of his that loves him well, you say—?

SHAKESPEARE. Too well!

HENSLOWE.   Why, man, it's common! Or too light, too low,
> Not once in a golden age love's scale trims level.

SHAKESPEARE. I read of lovers once in Italy—

HENSLOWE. You'll write of lovers too, not once nor twice.

SHAKESPEARE. Their scales were level ere they died of love,
> In Italy—

HENSLOWE. But if instead they had lived—in Stratford—there'd have been such a see-saw in six months as—

SHAKESPEARE. As what?

HENSLOWE. As there has been, eh?

> "See-saw! Margery Daw!
> She sold her bed to lie upon straw."

And so—poor Margery! Though she counts me an enemy—poor Margery!

SHAKESPEARE. What help for Margery—and her Jack?

HENSLOWE. None, friend, in Stratford.

SHAKESPEARE. Do I not know it?

HENSLOWE. Then—tell Margery!

SHAKESPEARE. Deaf, deaf!

HENSLOWE.   Not if you tell her how all heels in London
> (And the Queen dances!)
> So trip to the Stratford tune that I hot-haste
> Am sent to fetch the fiddler—

SHAKESPEARE.   Man, is it true?
     True that the Queen—?
HENSLOWE.   I say—tell Margery!
What! is she a woman, a wife, and will not further her man? I say
to you—tell Margery, as I tell you—
     SHAKESPEARE. You do?
     HENSLOWE. I do. I do tell you that if you can come away with us
now with your 'Dream' in your pocket, and teach it to us and
learn of us while you teach, and strike London in time for the Queen's
birthday—I tell you and I tell her, Jack's a made man. See what
Margery says to that, and give me the answer, stay or come, as I
pass here to-night! And now let me go; for if I do not soon whip
my company clear of apple-juice and apple-bloom, clear, that is to
say, of Stratford wine and Stratford women, we shall *not* pass here
to-night. [*He goes out.*]
     SHAKESPEARE. To-night! [*Calling*] Anne! Anne! [*He walks
up and down.*] Oh, to be one of them to-night on the silver road—
to smell the steaming frost and listen to men's voices and the ring of
iron on the London road! [*Calling*] Anne!
     ANNE [*entering*]. You called? He's gone? You're angry? Oh,
                    not now,
               No anger now; for, Will, to-night in the sky,
               Our sky, a new star shines.
SHAKESPEARE.   What's that? You know?
ANNE.   I know, and oh, my heart sings.
SHAKESPEARE.   Anne, dear Anne,
               You know? No frets? You wish it? Oh,
                    dear Anne,
               How did you guess and know?
ANNE.   My mother told me.
SHAKESPEARE.   She heard us? Did she hear—they've read the
                    play,

And the Queen's asked for me! London, Anne!
   London!
I'll send you London home, my lass, by the post—
Such frocks and fancies! London! London,
   Anne!
And you, you know? and speed me hence? By
   God,
That's my own wife at last, all gold to me
And goodness! Anne, be better to me still
And help me hence to-night!

ANNE.   It dips, it dies,
A night-light, Mother, and no star. I grope
Giddily in the dark.

SHAKESPEARE.   What did she tell you?
ANNE. No matter. Oh, it earns not that black look.
London? the Queen? I'll help you, oh, be
   sure!
Too glad to see you glad.

SHAKESPEARE.   Anne, it's good-bye
To Stratford till the game's won.

ANNE.   What care I
So you are satisfied? The farm must go—
That's little—

SHAKESPEARE.   Must it go?
ANNE.   Dreamer, how else
Shall we two live in London?

SHAKESPEARE.   *We,* do you say?
They'd have me travel with them—a rough life—
ANNE. I care not!
SHAKESPEARE.   —and you're ailing.
ANNE.   Better soon.
SHAKESPEARE. You'll miss your mother.

ANNE. Mothers everywhere
Will help a girl. I'm strong.

SHAKESPEARE. It will not do!
I have my world to learn, and learn alone.
I will not dangle at your apron-strings.

ANNE. I'll be no tie. I'll be your follower
And scarce your wife; but let me go with you!

SHAKESPEARE. If you could see but once, once, with my eyes!

ANNE. Will! let me go with you!

SHAKESPEARE. I tell you—no!
Leave me to go my way and rule my life
After my fashion! I'll not lean on you
Because you're seven years wiser.

ANNE. That too, O God!

SHAKESPEARE. And if I hurt you—for I know I do,
I'm not so rapt—think of me, if you can,
As a man stifled that wildly throws his arms,
Raking the air for room—for room to breathe,
And so strikes unaware, unwillingly,
His lover!

ANNE. I could sooner think of you
Asleep, and I beside you with the child,
And all this passion ended, as it must,
In quiet graves; for we have been such lovers
As there's no room for in the human air
And daylight side of the grass. What shall I do?
And how live on? Why did you marry me?

SHAKESPEARE. You know the why of that.

ANNE. Too well we know it,
I and the child. You have well taught this fool
That thought a heart of dreams, a loving heart,
A soul, a self resigned, could better please

Than the blind flesh of a woman; for God knows
Your self drew me, the folded man in you,
Not, not the boy-husk.

SHAKESPEARE.   Yet the same God knows
When folly was, you willed it first, not I.

ANNE.   Old! Old as Adam! and untrue, untrue!
Why did you come to me at Shottery,
Out of your way, so often? laugh with me
Apart, and answer for me as of right,
As if you knew me better (ah, it was sweet!)
Than my own brothers? And on Sunday eves
You'd wait and walk with me the long way home
From church, with me alone, the foot-path way,
Across the fields where wild convolvulus
Strangles the corn—

SHAKESPEARE.   Strangles the corn indeed!

ANNE.   —and still delay me talking at the stile,
Long after curfew, under the risen moon.
Why did you come? Why did you stay with
     me,
To make me love, to make me think you loved
     me?

SHAKESPEARE.   Oh, you were easy, cheap, you flattered me.

ANNE [crying out].   I did not.

SHAKESPEARE.   Why, did you not look at me
As I were God? And for a while I liked it.
It fed some weed in me that since has withered;
For now I like it not, nor like you for it!

ANNE.   That is your fate, you change, you must ever be
     changing,
You climb from a boy to a man, from a man to
     a god.

And the god looks back on the man with a smile,
 and the man on the boy with wonder;
But I, I am woman for ever: I change not at all.
You hold out your hands to me—heaven: you
 turn from me—hell;
But neither the hell nor the heaven can change
 me: I love you: I change not at all.

SHAKESPEARE. All this leads not to London, and for London
I am resolved: if not to-night—

ANNE.   To-night?

SHAKESPEARE. As soon as maybe. When the child is born—
When will the child be born?

ANNE.   Soon, soon—

SHAKESPEARE.   How soon?

ANNE. I think—I do not know—

SHAKESPEARE.   In March?

ANNE.   Who knows?

SHAKESPEARE. Did you not tell me March?

ANNE.   Easter—

SHAKESPEARE.   That's May!

It should be March.

ANNE.   It—should be—March—

SHAKESPEARE.   Why, Anne?

ANNE. Stay with me longer! Wait till Whitsuntide,
Till June, till summer comes, and if, when you
 see
Your own son, still you'll leave us, why, go then!
But sure, you will not go.

SHAKESPEARE.   Summer? Why summer?
It should be spring, not summer—

ANNE.   I'll not bear
These questions, like coarse fingers, prying out

My secrets.

SHAKESPEARE.   Secrets?

ANNE.   Secrets? I? I've none—
I never meant—I know not why the word
Came to me, "secret." Yet you're all secret
        thoughts
And plans you do not share. Why should not I
Be secret, if I choose? But see, I'll tell you
All, all—some other time—were there indeed
A thing to tell—

SHAKESPEARE.   When will the child be born?

ANNE.   If it were—June? My mother said to-day
It might be June—July— This woman's talk
Is not for you—

SHAKESPEARE.   July?

ANNE.   Oh, I must laugh
Because you look and look—don't look at me!
June! May! I swear it's May! I said the
        spring,
And May is still the girlhood of the year.

SHAKESPEARE.   July! A round year since you came to me!
Then—when you came to me, in haste, afraid,
All tears, and clung to me, and white-lipped swore
You had no friend but Avon if I failed you,
It was a lie?

ANNE.   Don't look at me!

SHAKESPEARE.   No need?
You forced me with a lie?

ANNE.   Now there is—now!

SHAKESPEARE.   You locked me in this prison with a lie?

ANNE.   I loved you.

SHAKESPEARE.   And you lied to me—

ANNE.   To hold you.
I couldn't lose you. I was mad with pain.

SHAKESPEARE. Are you so weak,
So candle-wavering, that a gust of pain
Could snuff out honour?

ANNE.   'Ware this hurricane
Of pain! The deserts heed it not, nor rocks,
Nor the perpetual sea; but oh, the fields
Where barley grows and small beasts hide, they
      fear—
And haggard woods that feel its violent hand
Entangled in their hair and wrestling, shriek
Crashing to ruin. What shall their pensioners
Do now, the rustling mice, the anemones,
The whisking squirrels, ivies, nightingales,
The hermit bee whose summer goods were stored
In a south bank? How shall the small things
      stand
Against the tempest, against the cruel sun
That stares them, homeless, out of countenance,
Through the day's heats?

SHAKESPEARE.   Coward! They see the sun
Though they die seeing, and the wider view,
The vast horizons, the amazing skies
Undreamed before.

ANNE.   I cannot see so far.
I want my little loves, I want my home.
My life is rooted up, my prop is gone,
And like a vine I lie upon the ground,
Muddied and broken.

SHAKESPEARE.   I could be sorry for you
Under the heavy hand of God or man

But your own hand has slain yourself and me.
Woman, the shame of it, to trap me thus,
Knowing I never loved you!

ANNE.   Oh, for a month—
In the spring, in the long grass, under the apple-
            trees—

SHAKESPEARE. I never loved you.

ANNE.   Think, when I hurt my hand
With the wild rose, it was then you said "Dear
            Anne!"

SHAKESPEARE. I have forgotten.

ANNE.   On Midsummer Eve—
There was a dream about a wood you told me,
Me—not another—

SHAKESPEARE.   I was drunk with dreams
That night.

ANNE.   That night, that night you loved me, Will!
Oh, never look at me and say—that night,
Under the holy moon, there was no love!

SHAKESPEARE. You knew it was not love.

ANNE.   O God, I knew,
And would not know! You never came again.
I hoped. I prayed. I hoped. I loved you so.
You never came.
And must I go to you? I was ashamed.
Yet in the wood I waited, waited, Will,
Night after night I waited, waited, Will,
Till shame itself was swallowed up in pain,
In pain of waiting, and—I went to you.

SHAKESPEARE. That lie upon those loving lips?

ANNE.   That lie.

SHAKESPEARE. There was no child?

ANNE.   The hope, the hope of children,
To bind you to me—a true hope to hold you—
No lie—a little lie—I loved you so—
Scarcely a lie—a promise to come true
Of gifts between us and a love to come.

SHAKESPEARE. You're mad! You're mad!

ANNE.   I was mad. I am sane.
I am blind Samson, shaking down the house
Of torment on myself as well as you.

SHAKESPEARE. What gain was there? What gain?

ANNE.   What gain but you?
The sight of your face and the sound of your foot
    on the stair,
And your casual word to a stranger—"This is my
    wife!"
For the touch of my hand on your arm, as a
    right, when we walked with the neighbours:
For the son, for the son on my heart, with your
    smile and your frown:
For the loss of my name in the name that you
    gave when you said to him—"Mother! your
    mother!"
For your glance at me over his head when he
    brought us his toys or his tears:
Have pity! Have pity! Have pity! for these
    things I did it.

SHAKESPEARE. Words! Words! You lied to me. Go your
    own road!
I know you not.

ANNE.   But I, but I know you.
Have I not learned my god's face? Have I not
    seen

The great dreams cloud it, as the ships of the sky
Darken the river? Has not the wind struck home,
The following chill wind that stirs all straws
Of omen? You're to be great, God pity you!
I'm your poor village woman; but I know
What you must learn and learn, and shriek to God
To spare you learning, if you will be great,
Singing to men and women across fields
Of years, and hearing answer as they reap,
Afar, the centuried fields, "He knew, he knew!"
How will they listen to you—voice that cries
"Right's right! Wrong's wrong! For every sin a stone!
"Ye shall not plead to any god or man—
" 'I flinched because the pain was very great,'
" 'I fell because the burden bore me down,'
" 'Hungry, I stole.' " O boy, ungrown, at judgment,
How will they listen? What? I lied? Oh, blind!
When I, your own, show you my heart of hearts,
A book for you to read all women by,
Blindly you turn my page with—"Here are lies!"

SHAKESPEARE.   Subtle enough—and glitter may be gold
In women's eyes—you say so—though to a man,
Boy rather (boy, you called me) lies are lies,
Base money, though you rub 'em till they shine,
Ill money to buy love with; but—I care not!
So be at ease! My love's not confiscate,
For none was yours to forfeit. Faith indeed,
A weakling trust is gone, for though you irked me

I thought you honest and so bore much from you—
Your jealous-glancing eye, officious hand
Meddling my papers, fool's opinion given
Unasked when strangers spoke with me, and
          laughter
Suddenly checked as if you feared a blow
As a dog does—it made me mad!

ANNE.   Go on!

SHAKESPEARE.   For when did I use you ill?

ANNE.   Go on!

SHAKESPEARE.   What need?
All's in a word—your ever-presence here
As if you'd naught in life to do but watch me—

ANNE.   Go on!

SHAKESPEARE.   All this, I say, I bore, because at heart
I did believe you loved me. Well—it's gone!
And I go with it—free, a free man, free!
Anne! for that word I could forgive you all
And go from you in peace.

ANNE [catching at his arm].   You shall not go!

SHAKESPEARE.   Shall not? This burr—how impudent it clings!

ANNE.   You have not heard me—

SHAKESPEARE.   Let me go, I say!
My purse, my papers—

ANNE.   Will!

SHAKESPEARE.   Talk to the walls,
For I hear nothing!

ANNE.   Why, a murderess
Has respite in my case—and I—and I—
What have I done but love you, when all's said?
You will not leave me now, now when that lie
Is certain truth at last, and in me sleeps

Like God's forgiveness? For I felt it stir
When you were angry—I was angry too,
My fault, all mine—but I was sick and faint
And frightened, so I railed, because no word
Matched with the strong need in me suddenly
For gentlest looks and your beloved arms
About this body changed and shaking so;
But why I knew not. But my mother knew
And told me.

SHAKESPEARE.   O wise mother!
ANNE.   Will, it's true!
SHAKESPEARE.   Practice makes perfect, as we wrote at school!
ANNE.   I swear to you—
SHAKESPEARE.   As then you swore to me.
Not twice, not twice, my girl!
ANNE.   O God, God Son!
Pitiful God! If there be other lives,
As I have heard him say, as his books say,
In other bodies, for Your Mother's sake
And all she knows (God, ask her what she knows!)
Let me not be a woman! Let me be
Some twisting worm on a hook, or fish they catch
And fling again to catch another year,
Or otter trapped and broiled in the sun three
        days,
Or lovely bird whose living wing men tear
From its live body, or of Italy
Some peasant's drudge-horse whipped upon its
        eyes,
Or let me as a heart-burst, screaming hare
Be wrenched in two by slavering deaths for
        sport;

But let me not again be cursed a woman
Surrendered to the mercy of her man!

> *She sinks down in a crouching heap by
> the hearth. There has been a sound of many
> voices drawing nearer, and as she ceases
> speaking, the words of a song become clear.*

THE PLAYERS [*singing*].   Come with us to London,
                    Folly, come away!
                  We'll make your fortune
                    On a summer day.
                  Leave your sloes and mulberries!
                  There are riper fruits than these,
                    In London, in London,
                    Oh, London Town!
                    For winds will blow
                    And barley grow
                    Without you, without you,
                  And the world get on without you—
                    Oh, London Town!

> *The voices drop to a low hum.* HENSLOWE
> *thrusts his head in at the window.*

HENSLOWE.   The sun's down. The sky's as yellow as a London
fog. Well, what's it to be?

SHAKESPEARE.   London! The future in a golden fog!

HENSLOWE.   Come then!

SHAKESPEARE.   I'll fetch my bundle. Wait for me! What
                    voices?

HENSLOWE.   The rest of us, the people of the plays.
                    We're all here waiting for you.

SHAKESPEARE.   Come in, all! all!

HENSLOWE.   Does your wife say to us—"Come in!"?

SHAKESPEARE. What wife?

He hurries up the stairs and disappears.

HENSLOWE [*opening the outer door*].

May we come in?

ANNE. You heard him.

HENSLOWE. We ask you.

ANNE. It's his house.

HENSLOWE [*humming*]. While fortune waits
Within the gates
Of London, of London—
He must be quick!

ANNE. Am *I* to tell him so?

HENSLOWE. The new moon's up and reaping in a sky
Like corn—that's frost! A bitter travelling
night
Before us—

ANNE [*going to the window*].
So it is.

HENSLOWE. Not through the glass!
You'll buy ill luck of the moon.

ANNE. I bought ill fortune
Long months ago under the shifty moon,
I saw her through the midnight glass of the air
Milky with light, when trees my casement were,
And little twigs the leads that held my pane.
I'm out of luck for ever.

HENSLOWE. Did I not tell you you feared your fortune? But
there are some in the company can tell you a better, if you'll let
'em in.

THREE PLAYERS IN MASKS [*tapping at the window*].

Let us in! Let us in! Let us in!

ANNE.   I will not let you in. Wait for your fellow
       On the high road! He'll come to you soon
       enough.
         She turns from them and seats herself by
         the fire.

A PLAYER [*dressed as a king, over* HENSLOWE'S *shoulder*]. Are we
never to come in? It's as cold as charity since the sun set.

ANNE. It's no warmer here.

A CHILD [*poking his head under the* PLAYER'S *arm*]. I can't feel
my fingers. [ANNE *looks at him. Her face changes.*]

ANNE.   If the fire warms you, you may warm yourselves.
          THE PLAYERS *stream in.*
       It does not warm me. Look! It cannot warm
       me.
         She thrusts her hand into the flame.

HENSLOWE. God's sake!
         He pulls her back. THE PLAYERS *stare*
         and whisper together.

ANNE.   Eyes! Needle eyes! Why do you stare and
       point?
       Like you I would have warmed myself. Vain,
       vain!
       It's a strange hearth. You players are the first
       It ever warmed or welcomed. Charity?
       Who said it—"Cold as charity"? That's love!
       But there's no love here. Baby, stay away!
       You'll freeze less out in churchyard night than
       here,
       For here's not even charity.

THE CHILD [*warming his hands*]. I'm not a baby. I'm nearly
eleven. I've played children's parts for years. I'm getting warmer.
Are you?

ANNE. No.

CHILD. I like this house. I'd like to stay here. I suppose there are things in that cupboard?

THE KING [overhearing]. Now, now!

CHILD. That's my father. He's a king this week. He's only a duke as a rule. Are there apples in that cupboard? Will you give me one?

ANNE *goes to the cupboard and takes out an apple.*

ANNE. Will you give me a kiss?

CHILD. For my apple?

ANNE. No, for love.

CHILD. I don't love you.

ANNE. For luck, then.

CHILD. You told him you'd got no luck.

ANNE. Won't you give me a kiss?

CHILD. If you like. Don't hold me so tight. Is it true you've no luck? Shall I tell your fortune?

ANNE. Can you?

CHILD. O yes! I've watched the Fates do it in the new play. It's Orpheus and—it's a long name. But she's his lost wife. Give me a handkerchief! That's for a grey veil. [*Posing.*] Now say to me—"Who are you?"

ANNE. Who are you?

CHILD [*posing*]. Fate! Now you must say—"Whose fate?"

ANNE. Whose?

CHILD. Oh, then I lift the veil and you scream. [*Stamping his foot.*] Scream!

ANNE. Why, baby?

CHILD [*frowning*]. At my dreadful face. [*But he begins to laugh in spite of himself.*]

ANNE [*her face hidden*]. Oh, child! Oh, child!

CHILD. That's right! That's the way she cries in the play. You see the man goes down to hell to find his wife, and the Fates show her what's going to happen while she's waiting for him. She's in hell already, waiting and waiting. It takes years to travel through hell. That's her talking to the old man in rags and a crown.

ANNE. Who's he?

CHILD. Oh, he's a poor old king whose daughters beat him. He isn't in this play. Well, when Orpheus gets to hell—I lead him there, you know—

ANNE. A babe in hell—a babe in hell—

CHILD. I'm the little god of love. I wear a crown of roses and wings. They do tickle. Soon I'll be too big. So he and I go to the three Fates to get back his wife. She isn't pretty in that act. She's all white and dead round her eyes—like you.

ANNE. Does he find her?

CHILD. After he sings his beautiful song he does. Everybody has to listen when he sings. Even the big dog lies down. Your husband made us a nice catch about it yesterday. I like your husband. I'm glad he's coming with us. Are you coming with us?

ANNE. No.

CHILD. It's a pity. If you were a man you could act in the company. But women can't act. Even Orpheus' wife is a boy really. So are the three Fates. They're friends of mine. Would you like to talk to them, the way we do in the play? Come on! I go first, you see. You must say just what I tell you.

> *He takes her hands and pulls her to her feet. She stares, bewildered, for the room has grown dim. The dying fire shines upon the shifting, shadowy figures of the* PLAYERS. *The crowd grows larger every moment and is thickest at the foot of the stairs.* SHAKESPEARE *is seen coming down them.*

ANNE. The room's so full. I'm frightened. Who are all these people?

CHILD. Hush! We're in hell. These are all the dead people
We bring 'em to life.

ANNE. Who? We?

CHILD. I and the singer. Look, there's your husband coming down
the stairs! That's just the way Orpheus comes down into hell.

ANNE. Will! Will!

CHILD. Hush! You mustn't talk.

ANNE. But it's all dreams—it's all dreams.

CHILD. It's the players.

SHAKESPEARE [*among the shadows*].

                    Let me pass!

THE SHADOWS.   Pay toll!

SHAKESPEARE.   How, pay it?

A SHADOW.   Tell my story?

ANOTHER.   And mine!

ANOTHER.   And mine!

ANOTHER.   And mine!

A ROMAN WOMAN.

                    Pluck back my dagger first and tell my story!

A DROWNED GIRL. Oh, listen, listen, listen, I've forgotten my own
story. It's a very sad one. Remember for me!

SHAKESPEARE.   I will remember. Let me pass!

A TROJAN WOMAN [*kissing him*].   Here's pay!

A VENETIAN.   I died of love.

THE TROJAN WOMAN.   Kiss me and tell my story!

A MOOR.   Dead lips, dead lips!

A YOUNG MAN.   This is how Judas kissed.

A QUEEN.   My son was taken from me. Tell my story!

ANOTHER.   And mine!

ANOTHER.   And mine!

A YOUNG MAN.   That son am I!

TWO CHILDREN.   I—I—

A SOLDIER.   I killed a king.

A CROWNED SHADOW.   He killed me while I slept.

THE SHADOWS.   You shall not pass until you tell our story!

A GIRL DRESSED AS A BOY.

          I lived in a wood and laughed. Sing you my
               laughter
          When the sun shone!

SHAKESPEARE.   I'll sing it. Singing I go,
          What shall I find after the song is over?
          What shall I find after the way is clear?

AN OLD MAN, A JEW.

          Gold and gold and gold—

A CLOWN.   And a grave untended—

A MAN IN BLACK.   Heartbreak—

TWO COUSINS.   A friend or two—

A ROMAN WITH LAURELS.   Oh, sing my story
          Before I had half-way climbed to the nearest star
          My ladder broke.

SHAKESPEARE.   I'll tell all time that story.

THE ROMAN.   The stars are dark, seen close.

SHAKESPEARE.   I'll say it.

THE ROMAN.   Pass!

AN EGYPTIAN [holding a goblet].

          He shall not pass. Drink! There are pearls
               in the cup.

A GIRL, A VERONESE [taking it from her].

          No—sleep!

A MAN [with a wand].   Dreams!

THE KING IN RAGS.   Frenzy!

A NUN.   Sacrament!

A DRUNKARD.   A jest!

A ROMAN WIFE.   Here's coals for bread.

THE EGYPTIAN [*A man in armour has flung his arm about her neck*].   Eat, drink and pass again
To the lost sunshine and the passionate nights,
And tell the world our story!

SHAKESPEARE.   Let me go!

ALL THE SHADOWS.
Never, never, never! To the end of time we follow,
Follow, follow, follow!

SHAKESPEARE.   Threads and floating wisps
Of being, how they fasten like a cloud
Of gnats upon me, not to be shaken off
Unsatisfied—

THE SHADOWS.   Sing! Sing!
There is a strain of music: the crowd hides SHAKESPEARE: *the three masked players have drifted free of the turmoil.*

CHILD [*delighted*]. He does it quite as well as Orpheus.

ANNE. Who are these dreams?

CHILD. The people of the plays. And there are the Fates at last! That's the end of my part. Now you must talk to them till your husband comes. He comes when you scream.
He picks up his bow and runs away.

ANNE.   Come back! Stay by me!

CHILD [*laughing*].   Play your part alone.
He is lost in the crowd. THE MASKS *have drawn near. The first is small and closely veiled and carries the distaff. The second is tall: part of her face shows white: her hands are empty. The third is bowed and crowned: she carries the shears.*

ANNE.   These are all dreams or I am mad. Who are
you?

FIRST MASK.   His fate. I hold the thread.

ANNE.   I'll see you!

FIRST MASK.   No!

As she retreats the SECOND MASK *takes the
distaff from her.*

SECOND MASK.   I tangle it.

ANNE.   Who are you?

SECOND MASK.   Fate! his fate!

ANNE.   Drop the bright mask and let me see!

The SECOND MASK *drops her veil and
shows the face of a dark lady.*

It needs not!

I knew, I knew! Barren the ground beneath,
No flowers, no fruit, spent arrows—

The SECOND MASK *makes way for the*
THIRD *who takes the tangle from her. The*
SECOND MASK *glides away.*

Not the shears!

THIRD MASK [*winding the thread*].

Not yet!

ANNE.   Who are you?

THIRD MASK.   Fate! his fate!

ANNE.   A crown!

My snake should know its fellow—is it so?

The mask is lifted and reveals the face of
ELIZABETH.

I do not fear the Queen—

THIRD MASK.   Take back the thread!

She gives the distaff to the FIRST MASK *who
has reappeared beside her and glides away.*

ANNE.   But you I fear, O shrinking fate! what fate?
            What first and last fate? Show me your face, I
            say!

                 *She tears off the mask. The face revealed
               is the face of* ANNE. *She screams.*

            Myself! I saw myself! Will! Will!

                 THE CHILD *kneeling at the hearth stirs
               the fire and a bright flame shoots up that
               lights the whole room. It is empty save for
               the few players gathering together their
               bundles and* SHAKESPEARE *who has hurried
               to* ANNE. *His hand, gripping her shoulder,
               steadies her as she sways.*

SHAKESPEARE.   Still railing?

CHILD [*to his father*]. She's a poor frightened lady and she cried.
I like her.

ANNE.   Gone! Gone! Where are they? Call them
            back! I saw—

SHAKESPEARE.   What folly! These are players and my friends;
            You could have given them food at least and
            served them.

ANNE.   I saw—I saw—

HENSLOWE [*coming up to them*]. So, are you ready? The moon is
high: we must be going.

SHAKESPEARE.   I'll follow instantly.

                 THE PLAYERS *trail out by twos and threes.
               They pass the window and repass it on the
               further side of the hedge. They are a black,
               fantastic frieze upon the yellow, winter sky.
               HENSLOWE goes first: the king's crown is
               crooked, and the child is riding on his back:
               the masks come last.*

THE PLAYERS [*singing*]. Come away to London,
                        Folly, come away!
                    You'll make your fortune
                        Thrice in a day.
                    Paddocks leave and winter byres,
                    London has a thousand spires,
                        A-chiming, a-rhyming,
                        Oh, London Town!
                        The snow will fall
                        And cover all
                        Without you, without you,
                    And the world get on without you—
                        Oh, London Town!
                        SHAKESPEARE *goes hurriedly to the table
                        and picks up his books.*

ANNE.   Will!
SHAKESPEARE.   For your needs
                    You have the farm. Farewell!
ANNE [*catching at his arm*].   For pity's sake!
                    I'm so beset with terrors not my own—
                    What have you loosed upon me? I'll not be left
                    In this black house, this kennel of chained grief,
                    This ghost-run. Take me with you ! No, stay
                        by me !
                    These are but dreams of evil. Shall we not wake
                    Drowsily in a minute ? Oh, bless'd waking
                    To peace and sunshine and no evil done !
                    Count out the minute—
SHAKESPEARE.   If ever I forget
                    The evil done me, I'll forget the spring,
                    And Avon, and the blue ways of the sky,
                    And my own mother's face.

ANNE.   Do I say "forget"?
I say "remember"! When you've staked all, all,
Upon your one throw—when you've lost—re-
     member!
And done the evilest thing you would not do,
Self-forced to the vile wrong you would not do,
Me in that hour remember!

SHAKESPEARE.   Let me go!
ANNE [*she is on the ground, clinging to him*].
Remember! See, I do not pray "forgive"!
Forgive? Forgiving is forgetting—no,
Remember me! Remember, when your sun
Blazes the noon down, that my sun is set,
Extinct and cindered in a bitter sea,
And warm me with a thought. For we are bound
Closer than love or chains or marriage binds:
We went by night and each in other's heart
Sowed tares, sowed tears. Husband, when
     harvest comes,
Of all your men and women I alone
Can give you comfort, for you'll reap my pain
As I your loss. What other knows our need?
Dear hands, remember, when you hold her, thus,
Close, close—

SHAKESPEARE.   Let go my hands!
ANNE.   —and when she turns
To stone, to a stone, to an unvouchsafing stone
Under your clutch—

SHAKESPEARE.   You rave!
ANNE.   —loved hands, remember
Me unloved then, and how my hands held you!
And when her face—for I am prophecy—

When her lost face, the woman I am not,
Stares from the page you toil upon, thus, thus,
In a glass of tears, remember then that thus,
No other way,
I see your face between my work and me,
Always!

SHAKESPEARE.　　　　Make end and let me go!

ANNE [*she has risen*].　　　　　　　　Why, go!
But mock me not with any "Let me go"!
I do not hold you.　Ah, but when you're old
(You will be old one day, as I am old
Already in my heart), too weary-old
For love, hate, pity, anything but peace,
When the long race, O straining breast! is won,
And the bright victory drops to your outstretched
　hand,
A windfall apple, not worth eating, then
Come back to me—

SHAKESPEARE [*at the door*].　　　Farewell!

ANNE.　　　　　　　　　—when all your need
Is hands to serve you and a breast to die on,
Come back to me—

SHAKESPEARE.　　　　　　Never in any world!

　　　　*He goes out as the last figure passes the
　　　　window, and disappears.*

THE PLAYERS' VOICES [*dying away*].

　　　　　　For snow will fall
　　　　　　And cover all
　　　　　　Without you, without you—
　　　　The words are lost.

SHAKESPEARE [*joyfully*].　　Ah!　London Town!

　　　　He is seen an instant, a silhouette with

outstretched arms. Then he, too, disappears and there is a long silence. A cold wind blows in through the open door. The room is quite dark and the fire has fallen to ashes.

ANNE [*crying out suddenly*].

The years—the years before me!

MRS. HATHAWAY [*calling*].   Anne! Where's Anne?

She comes in at the side door.

Anne! Anne! Where are you? Why, what do you here,

In the cold, in the dark, and all alone?

ANNE.   I wait.

THE CURTAIN FALLS.

ACT II.

SCENE I.

A room at the Palace. ELIZABETH *sits at a working table. She is upright, vigorous, with an ivory white skin and piercing eyes. Her hair is dark red and stiffly dressed. She is old, as an oak or a cliff or a cathedral is old—there is no frailty of age in her. Her gestures are measured, she moves very little, and frowns oftener than she smiles, but her smile, when it does come, is kindly. Her voice is strong, rather harsh, but clear. She speaks her words like a scholar, but her manner is that of a woman of the world, shrewd and easy. Her dress is a black-green brocade, stiff with gold and embroidered with coloured stones. Beside her stands* HENSLOWE, *ten years older, stouter and more prosperous. In the background* MARY FITTON, *a woman of twenty-six, sits at the virginals, fingering out a tune very faintly and lightly. She is taller than* ELIZABETH, *pale, with black hair, a smiling mouth and brilliant eyes. She is quick and graceful as a cat, and her voice is the voice of a singer, low and full. She wears a magnificent black and white dress with many pearls. A red rose is tucked behind her ear.*

ELIZABETH. Money, money! Always more money! Henslowe, you're a leech! And I'm a Gammer Gurton to let myself be bled. Let the public pay!

HENSLOWE. Madam, they'll do that fast enough if we may call ourselves Your Majesty's Players.

ELIZABETH. No, no, you're not yet proven. What do you give me? Good plays enough, but what great play? What has England, what have I, to match against them when they talk to me of their Tasso, their Petrarch, their Rabelais—of Divine Comedies and the plays of Spain? Are we to climb no higher than the Germans with their 'Ship of Fools'?

HENSLOWE. 'The Faery Queen'?

ELIZABETH. Unfinished.

HENSLOWE. Green—Peele—Kyd—Webster—

ELIZABETH. Stout English names—not names for all the world. I will pay you no more good English pounds a year and fib to my treasurer to account for them. You head a deputation, do you? You would call yourselves the Queen's Players, and mount a crown on your curtains? Give me a great play then—a royal play—a play to set against France and Italy and Spain, and you can have your patent.

HENSLOWE. There's 'Tamburlaine'!

ELIZABETH. A boy's glory, not a man's.

HENSLOWE. 'Faust' and 'The Jew of Malta'!

ELIZABETH. I know them.

HENSLOWE. He'll do greater things yet.

ELIZABETH. Do you believe that, Henslowe?

HENSLOWE. No, Madam.

ELIZABETH. Then why do you lie to me?

HENSLOWE. Madam, I mark time. I have my man; but he is not yet ripe.

ELIZABETH. How long have you served me, Henslowe?

HENSLOWE. Twelve years.

ELIZABETH. How often have you come to me in those twelve years?

HENSLOWE. Four times, Madam!

ELIZABETH. Have I helped or hindered?

HENSLOWE.　I confess it, Madam, I have lived on your wits.

ELIZABETH.　Then who's your man?

HENSLOWE.　You'll not trust me.　He has done little before the world.

ELIZABETH.　Shakespeare?

HENSLOWE.　Madam, you know everything.　Will you see him? He and Marlowe are among our petitioners.

ELIZABETH.　H'm! the Stratford boy!　I have not forgotten.

HENSLOWE.　Who could have promised better?　He came to town like a conqueror.　He took us all with his laughter.　You yourself, Madam—

ELIZABETH.　Yes, make us laugh and you may pick all pockets! He helped you to pick mine.

HENSLOWE.　So far good.　But he aims no higher.　Yet what he could do if he would!　I have a sort of love of him, Madam.　I found him: I taught him: I have daughters enough but no son.　I have wrestled with him like Jacob at Peniel, but when I think to conquer he tickles my rib and I laugh.　That's his weapon, Madam! With his laughter he locks the door of his heart against every man.

ELIZABETH.　And every woman?

HENSLOWE.　They say—no, Madam!

ELIZABETH.　Then we must find her.

HENSLOWE [with a glance at MARY FITTON].　They say she is found already.　But a court lady—and a player!　It's folly, Madam! Now Marlowe would shrug his shoulder and go elsewhere; but Shakespeare—there is about him in little and great a certain dogged and damnable constancy that wrecks all.　If he cannot have the moon for his supper, he will starve, Madam, whatever an old fool says to him.

ELIZABETH.　Then, Henslowe, we must serve him up the moon. Mary!

MARY [rising and coming down to them].　Madam?

ELIZABETH. Could you hear us?

MARY. I was playing the new song that the Earl set for you.

ELIZABETH. For me? But you heard?

MARY. Something of the talk, Madam!

ELIZABETH. You go to all the plays, do you not? Which is the coming man, Mary, Shakespeare or Marlowe?

MARY. If you ask me, Madam, I'm all for the cobbler's son.

HENSLOWE. Mistress Fitton should give us a sound reason if she have it, but she has none.

MARY. Only that I don't know Mr. Marlowe, and I know my little Shakespeare by heart. I'm an Athenian—I'm always asking for new tunes.

ELIZABETH. Which is Shakespeare? The youngster like a smoking lamp, all aflare?

MARY. No, Madam! That's Marlowe. Shakespeare's a lesser man.

HENSLOWE. A lesser man? Marlowe the lamp, say you?
He's conflagration, he's "Armada!" flashed
From Kent to Cornwall! But this lesser man,
He's the far world the beacons can outflare
One little hour, but, when their flame dies down,
High o'er the embers in the deep of night
Behold the star!

ELIZABETH. I forget if ever I saw him.

HENSLOWE. Madam, if ever you saw him, you would not forget—
A small, a proud head, like an Arab Christ,
And noble, madman's fingers, never still—
The face still though, mouth hid, the nostril wide,
And eyes like voices calling, shrill and sad,
Borne on hot winds from fairyland or hell;
Yet round the heavy lids a score of lines
All criss-cross crinkle like a score of laughs

That he has scribbled hastily down himself
With his quick fingers. No, not tall—

ELIZABETH.   But a man!
MARY.   Like other men.
ELIZABETH.   Ah?
MARY.   It was easy.
ELIZABETH.   Tell!
MARY.   He came like a boy to apples. Marlowe now—
ELIZABETH.   More than a man, less than a man, but not
                    As yet a man then? Well, I'll see your Shake-
                         speare:
                    Marlowe—some other time.
HENSLOWE.   I'll fetch him to you.

         HENSLOWE *goes out.*

ELIZABETH. To you, Mary—to you!

MARY. O Madam, spare me! It's a stiff instrument and once, I
think, has been ill-tuned.

ELIZABETH. Tune it afresh!

MARY. You wish that, Madam?

ELIZABETH. I wish it. Marlowe can wait—and Pembroke.

MARY. Madam?

ELIZABETH. I am blind, deaf, dumb, so long as you practise your
new tune. But the Earl of Pembroke goes to Ireland.

MARY. He's an old glove, Madam.

ELIZABETH. Young or old, not for your wearing. Strip your hand
and finger your new tune!

MARY. Now, Madam?

ELIZABETH. Why not? Why do I dress you and keep you at court?
Here's Spain in the ante-room and France on the stairs—am I to
keep them waiting while I humour a parcel of players?

MARY. Indeed, Madam, I wonder that you have spared half an
hour.

ELIZABETH. Wonder, Mary! Wonder! And when you know why I do what I do you shall be Queen instead of me. In the meantime you may learn the trade, if you choose. I give you a kingdom to rule in the likeness of a poor player. Let me see how you do it! Yet mark this—though with fair cheeks and black hair you may come by a coronet (but the Earl goes to Ireland) yet if you rule your kingdom by the glance of your eyes, you will lose it as other Maries have done.

MARY. I must reign in my own way—forgive me, Madam!—not yours.

ELIZABETH. Girl, do you think you could ever rule in mine? Well, try your way! But—between queens, Mary—one kingdom at a time!

ELIZABETH *goes out.*

MARY [*she sits on the table edge, swinging her pretty foot*]. So Pembroke goes to Ireland! Ay, and comes back, old winter! I can wait. And while I wait—Shakespeare! Will Shakespeare! O charity—I wish it were Marlowe! What did the old woman say? A kingdom in the likeness of a player. I wonder. Well, we'll explore. Yet I wish it were Marlowe. [SHAKESPEARE *enters.*] Ah! here comes poor Mr. Shakespeare looking for the Queen and finding—

SHAKESPEARE. The Queen!

MARY. Hush! Palace walls! Well, Mr. Shakespeare, what's the news?

SHAKESPEARE. Good, bad and indifferent.

MARY. Take the bad first.

SHAKESPEARE. The bad?—that I have not seen you some five weeks! The good—that I have now seen you some five seconds! The indifferent—that you do not care one pin whether I see you or not for the next five years!

MARY. Who told you that, Solomon?

SHAKESPEARE. I have had no answer to—

MARY. Five letters, seven sonnets, two catches and a roundelay!

SHAKESPEARE. Love's Labour Lost!

MARY. Ah, Mr. Shakespeare, you were not a Solomon then! There was too much Rosaline and too little Queen in that labour.

SHAKESPEARE. You're right! Solomon would have drawn all Rosaline and no Queen at all. I'll write another play!

MARY. It might pay you better than your sonnets.

SHAKESPEARE. Do you read them — Rosaline?

MARY. Most carefully, Mr. Shakespeare—on Saturday nights! Then I make up my accounts and empty my purse, and wonder—must I pawn my jewels? Then I cry. And then I read your latest sonnet and laugh again.

SHAKESPEARE. You should not laugh.

MARY. Why, is it not meant to move me?

SHAKESPEARE.   You should not laugh. I tell you such a thought,
                         Such fiery lava welling from a heart,
                         So crystalled in the wonder-working brain,
                         Mined by the soul and rough-cut into words
                         Fit for a poet's faceting and, last,
                         Strung on a string of gold by a golden tongue—
                         Why, such a thought is an immortal jewel
                         To gild you, living, in men's eyes, and after
                         To make you queen of all the unjewelled dead
                         Who bear not their least bracelet hence. For I,
                         Eternally I'd deck you, were you my own,
                         Would you but wear my necklaces divine,
                         My rings of sorcery, my crowns of song.
                         What chains of emeralds—did you but know!
                         My rubies, O my rubies could you but see!
                         And this one gem of wonder, pearl of pearls,
                         Hid in my heart for you, could you but take,
                         Would you but take—

MARY.   Open your heart!

SHAKESPEARE.   Not so.
The god who made it hath forgot the key,
Or lost or lent it.

MARY.   Heartless god! Poor heart!
Yet if this key—(is there indeed a key?)

SHAKESPEARE. No lock without a key, nor heart, nor heart.

MARY.   —were found one day and strung with other keys
Upon my ring?

SHAKESPEARE.   With other—?

MARY.   Keys of hearts!
What else?
Tucked in the casket where my mortals lie—
Sick pearl, flawed emerald, brooch or coronet—

SHAKESPEARE. God!

MARY.   Why, Jeweller?

SHAKESPEARE.   Then what they say—

MARY.   They say?
What do they say? And what care I? They say
Pembroke?

SHAKESPEARE.   They lie! You shall not speak. They lie!

MARY.   So little doubt—and you a man! It's new,
It's sweet. It will not last. We spoke of
    keys—
This heart-key, had I found it, would you buy?
Come, tempt me with immortal necklaces!
Come, purchase me with ornaments divine!

SHAKESPEARE. I love you—

MARY.   Well?

SHAKESPEARE.   I love you—

MARY.   Is that all?

SHAKESPEARE. I love you so.

MARY.   Why, that's a common cry,

I hear it daily, like the London cries,
"Old chairs to mend!" or "Sweet, sweet
lavender!"
Is this your string of pearls, sixteen a penny?

SHAKESPEARE. D'you laugh at me? I mean it.
MARY.   So do they all.
Buy! Buy my lavender! Lady, it's cheap—
It's sweet—new cut—I starve—for Christ's
sake, buy!
They mean it, all the hoarse-throat, hungry men
That sell me lavender, that sell me love.

SHAKESPEARE. I put my wares away. I do not sell.
MARY. O pedlar! I had half a mind to buy.
SHAKESPEARE. Too late.
MARY.   Open your pack again! What haste!
What—not a trinket left me, not a pin
For a poor lady? Does not the offer hold?

SHAKESPEARE. You did not close.
MARY.   I will.
SHAKESPEARE.   Withdrawn! Withdrawn!
MARY. Renew!
SHAKESPEARE.   Too late.
MARY.   You know your business best;
Yet—what care I?

SHAKESPEARE.   Or I? Yet—never again
To buy and sell with you!

MARY.   Never again!
Heigh-ho! I sighed, sir.

SHAKESPEARE.   Yes, I heard you sigh.
MARY. And smiled. At court, sir—
SHAKESPEARE.   Yes, they buy and sell
At court. But I know better—give and take!

MARY [*evading him*].

What will you give me if I let you take?

SHAKESPEARE. If you will come with me into my mind—
How shall I say it? Still you'll laugh at me!

MARY. Maybe!

SHAKESPEARE. My mind's not one room stored, but many,
A house of windows that o'erlook far gardens,
The hanging gardens of more Babylons
Than there are bees in a linden tree in June.
I'm the king-prisoner in his capital,
Ruling strange peoples of a world unknown,
Yet there come envoys from the untravelled lands
That fill my corridors with miracles
As it were tribute, secretly, by night;
And I wake in the dawn like Solomon,
To stare at peacocks, apes and ivory,
And a closed door.
And all these stores I give you for your own,
You shall be mistress of my fairy-lands,
I'll ride you round the world on the back of a
dream,
I'll give you all the stars that ever danced
In the sea o' nights,
If you will come into my mind with me,
If you will learn me—know me.

MARY. I do know you.
You are the quizzical Mr. Shakespeare of the 'Rose,' who never
means a word he says. I've heard of you. All trades hate you
because you are not of their union, and yet know the tricks of each
trade; but your own trade loves you, because you are content with a
crook in the lower branches when you might be top of the tree.
You write comedies, all wit and no wisdom, like a flower-bed raked

but not dug; but the high stuff of the others, their tragedies and lamentable ends, these you will not essay. Why not, Mr. Shakespeare of the fairy-lands?

SHAKESPEARE. Queen Wasp, I do not know.

MARY. King Drone, then I will tell you. You are the little boy at Christmas who would not play snap-dragon till the flames died down, and so was left at the end with a cold raisin in an empty dish. That's you, that's you, with the careful fingers and no good word in your plays for any woman. Run home, run home, there's no more to you!

SHAKESPEARE. D'you think so?

MARY. I think that I think so.

SHAKESPEARE. I'll show you.

MARY. What will you show me, Will?

SHAKESPEARE. Fairyland, and you and me in it. Will you believe in me then?

MARY. Not I, not I! I'm a woman of this world. Give me flesh and blood, not gossamer,

> Honey and heart-ache, and a lovers' moon.

SHAKESPEARE.   I read of lovers once in Italy—
> She was like you, such eyes of night, such hair.
> God took a week to make his world, but these
> In four short days made heaven to burn on earth
> Like a great torch; and when they died—

MARY.   They died?

SHAKESPEARE.   Like torches quenched in water, suddenly,
> Because they loved too well.

MARY.   Oh, write it down!
> Ah, could you, Will? I think you could not
> write it.

SHAKESPEARE.   I can write Romeo. Teach me Juliet!

MARY. I could if I would. Was that her name—Juliet?

SHAKESPEARE. Poor Juliet!

MARY. Not so poor if I know her. Oh, make that plain—she was not poor! And tell them, Will, tell all men and women—

SHAKESPEARE. What, my heart?

MARY. I will whisper it to you one day when I know you better. Oh, it'll be a play! Will you do it for me, Will? Will you write it for you and for me? Where do they live?

SHAKESPEARE. Verona. Italy.

MARY. Come to me daily! Read it to me scene by scene, line by line! How many acts?

SHAKESPEARE. The old five-branched candlestick.

MARY.   But a new flame! Will it take long to write? It must not.

SHAKESPEARE.   Shall not.

MARY.   What shall we call it, Will? The Tragical Discourse? The Famous End? The Lovers of Verona?

SHAKESPEARE.   No, no! Plain. Their two names married—Romeo and Juliet.

          As they lean towards each other still talking

THE CURTAIN FALLS.

ACT II.

Scene II.

The first performance of Romeo and Juliet: the end of the fourth
act. The curtain rises on a small bare dusty office, littered with
stage properties and dresses. When the door at the back of the
stage is open there is a glimpse of passage and curtains, and
moving figures, with now and then a flare of torchlight. There
is a continuous far-away murmur of voices and, once in a while,
applause. As the curtain goes up MARY FITTON is opening the
door to go out. SHAKESPEARE holds her back.

MARY. Let go! Let me go! I must be in front at the end of
that act. I must hear what the Queen will say to it.

SHAKESPEARE. But you'll come back?

MARY. That depends on what the Queen says. I've promised
you nothing if she damns it.

    The applause breaks out again.

SHAKESPEARE. Listen! Is it damned?

MARY. Sugar-sweet, isn't it? But that's nothing. That's the
mob. That's your friends. They'll clap *you*. But the Queen, if
she claps, claps your play.

SHAKESPEARE. Your play!

MARY. Is it mine? Earnest?

SHAKESPEARE. My earnest, but your play.

MARY. Well, good luck to my play!

SHAKESPEARE. Give me—

MARY. Oh, so it's not a free gift?

SHAKESPEARE. Give me a finger-tip of thanks!

MARY. In advance? Not I! But if the Queen likes it—I'm her obedient servant. If the Queen opens her hand I shan't shut mine. Where she claps once I'll clap twice. Where she gives you a hand to kiss, I'll give you— There! Curtain's down! I must go.

SHAKESPEARE. Mary!

MARY. Listen to it! Listen! Listen! This is better than any poor Mary.

> *She goes out. The door is left open. The applause breaks out again.*

SHAKESPEARE.   Is this the golden apple in my hand
At last?
How tastes it, heart, and is it sweet, is it sweet?
Sweeter than common apples? So many years
Of days I watched it grow and propped and
pruned,
Besought the sun and watered. O my tree
When the green broke! That was a morning hour.
Fool, so to long for fruit! Now the fruit's ripe.
The tree in spring was fairest, when it flowered,
And every petal held a drink of dew.
The bloom went long ago. Well, the fruit's here!
Hark!

> *The applause breaks out again.*

It goes well. Eat up your apple, man!
This is the hour, the hour! I'm the same man—
No better for it. When Marlowe praised me so
He meant it—meant it. I thought he laughed
at me
In his sleeve. Will Shakespeare! Romeo and
Juliet!
I made it—I! Indeed, indeed, at heart—

(I would not for the world they read my heart:
I'd scarce tell Mary) but indeed, at heart,
I know no song was ever sung before
Like this my lovely song. *I* made it—I!
It has not changed me. I'm the same small man,
And yet I made it! Strange!   [*A knock.*]

STAGE HAND [*putting in his head at the door*]. You'll not see anyone, sir, will you?

SHAKESPEARE. I told you already I'll come to the green-room when the show's over. I can see no stranger before.

STAGE HAND. So I've told her, sir, many times. But she says you will know her when you see her and she can't wait.

SHAKESPEARE. A lady?

STAGE HAND. No, no, sir, just a woman. I'll tell her to go away again.

SHAKESPEARE. Wait! Did she give no name?

STAGE HAND. Name of Hathaway, sir, from Stratford.

SHAKESPEARE. Anne! Bring her here! Bring her here quickly, privately. You should have told me sooner. Where does she wait? Did any see her? Did any speak with her? If anyone asks for me save Henslowe or Mr. Marlowe, I am gone, I am not in the theatre. What are you staring at? What are you waiting for? Bring her here!

STAGE HAND. Glad to be rid of her, sir! She has sat in the passage this hour to be tripped over, and nothing budges her. [*Calling*] Will you come this way—this way! [*He disappears.*]

SHAKESPEARE. Anne? Anne in London? What does Anne in London?

STAGE HAND [*returning*]. This way, this way! It's a dark passage. This way!

          MRS. HATHAWAY *comes in.*

SHAKESPEARE. Not Anne!

MRS. HATHAWAY. Is Mr. Shakespeare—? Will! 'Is it Will? Oh, how you're changed!

SHAKESPEARE. Ten years change a young man.

MRS. HATHAWAY. But not an old woman. I'm Anne's mother still.

SHAKESPEARE. I'm not so changed that I forget it. What do you want of me, Mrs. Hathaway?

MRS. HATHAWAY. I bring you news.

SHAKESPEARE. Good news?

MRS. HATHAWAY. It's as you take it.

SHAKESPEARE. Dead?

MRS. HATHAWAY. Is that good news, my half son? She is not so blessed.

SHAKESPEARE. I did not say it so. Is she with you?

MRS. HATHAWAY. No.

SHAKESPEARE. Did she send you? Oh, so she has heard of this business! It's like her to send you now. She is to take her toll of it, is she?

MRS. HATHAWAY. You are bitter, you are bitter! You are the east wind of your own spring sunshine. She has heard nothing of this business or of that—dark lady.

SHAKESPEARE. Take care!

MRS. HATHAWAY. I saw her come from this room—off her guard. I know how a woman looks when a man has pleased her. Oh, please her if you must! I am old. I do not judge. And I think you will not always. But that's not my news.

SHAKESPEARE. I can't hear it now. I am pressed. This is not every night. I'll see you to-morrow, not now.

MRS. HATHAWAY. My news may be dead to-morrow.

SHAKESPEARE. So much the better. I needn't hear it.

MRS. HATHAWAY. Son, son, son! You don't know what you say.

SHAKESPEARE. That is not my name. And I know well what I

say. You are my wife's mother and I'll not share anything of hers.
But if she needs money, I'll send it. To-night makes me a rich man.

MRS. HATHAWAY. Richer than you think—and to-morrow poorer,
if you do not listen to me.

There is a roar of applause.

SHAKESPEARE. Listen to you? Why should I listen to you? Can
you give me anything to better that?

MRS. HATHAWAY. But if she can? Fifty years I have learned
lessons in the world; but I never learned that a city was better than
green fields, friends better than a house-mate, or the works of a
man's hand more to him than the child of his own flesh.

SHAKESPEARE.   And have I learned it, I? Do I not know
              That when I left her I left all behind
              That was my right? See how I live my life—
              Married nor single, neither bond nor free,
              My future mortgaged for a roofless home!
              For though I love I must not say "I love you,
              Come to my hearth!" A child? I have no child:
              I hear no voice crying to me o' nights
              Out of the frost-bound dark. How can it cry
              Or smile at me until I give it lips?
              How can it clutch me till I give it hands?
              How can it be, until I give it leave?
              Small sparrow at the window-pane, a'cold,
              Begging your crumb of life from me, indeed
              I cannot let you in. Small love, small sweet,
              Look not so trustfully! You are not mine,
              Not mine, not anyone's. Away, unborn!
              Back to the womb of dreams, and never stir,
              Never again! How meek the small ghost fades,
              Reject and fatherless, that might have been
              My son!

MRS. HATHAWAY. Is it possible? Anne knew you best.
She said you did not know. Dear son, too soon
By two last months, yet by these months too late
After you left her, Hamnet, the boy, was born.

SHAKESPEARE. It is not true!

MRS. HATHAWAY. Ah, ah, she knew you best.
She said always, weeping she said always
You would not listen, though she sent you word;
But when the boy was grown she'd send the boy,
Then you would listen and come home, come home.
But now that web is tattered in its turn
By a cold wind, an out-of-season wind,
Tearing the silver webs, blacking the leaves
And shaking the first blossoms down too soon,
Too soon, too soon. He shivered and lay down
Among pinched violets and the wrack of spring;
But when the sky drew breath and April came,
And summer with tanned fingers, beckoning up
New flowers from the ground, still our flower
            drooped;
The sunlight hurt his eyes, his bed's too hot,
He drinks and will not eat: since Saturday
There's but one end.

SHAKESPEARE. What end?

MRS. HATHAWAY. You're stubborn as she.
She will not bow to it. Yet she sent me hither
To bring you home.

SHAKESPEARE. New witch-work!

MRS. HATHAWAY. Will you not come?

SHAKESPEARE. I will not.

MRS. HATHAWAY. Will you not come? She bade me say
That the boy cries for you—

SHAKESPEARE.   A lie! A gross lie!
He never called me father.

MRS. HATHAWAY.   That he does!
You are his Merlin and his Arthur too,
And God-Almighty Sundays. Thus it goes—
"My Father says—" and "When my Father
    comes—"
"I'll tell my Father!" To his mother's hand
He clings and whispers in his fever now,
With bright eyes wide—your eyes, son, your
    quick eyes—
That she shall fetch you (she? she cannot
    speak)
To bring him wonders home like Whittington,
(And where's your cat?) and tell the tales you
    know
Of Puck and witches, and the English kings,
To whistle down the birds as Orpheus did,
And for a silver penny pick the moon
From the sky's pocket, and buy him gingerbread—
And so he rambles on, breaking her heart
A second time, God help her!

SHAKESPEARE.   I will come.

A MAN'S VOICE [*off the stage*].
Shakespeare! Will Shakespeare! Call Will
    Shakespeare!

SHAKESPEARE [*to* MRS. HATHAWAY].   Here!
When do we start?

MRS. HATHAWAY.   The horses wait at the inn.

VOICE.   Will Shakespeare!

SHAKESPEARE.   Give me an hour. The bridge is nearer.
On London Bridge at midnight! I'll be there!

MRS. HATHAWAY. Not later, I warn you, if you'd see the child alive.

SHAKESPEARE. Fear not, I'll be there. D'you think so ill of me? I could have been a good father to my own son—if I had known. If I had known! This is a woman's way of enduring a wrong. Oh, dumb beast! Could she not send for me—send to me? Am I a monster that she could not come to me? "Buy him gingerbread"! To send me no word till he's dying! Would any she-devil in hell do so to a man? Dying? I tell you he shall live and not die. There was a man once fought death for a friend and held him. Can I not fight death for my own son? Can I not beat death off for an hour, for a little hour, till I have kissed my only son?

MARLOWE'S VOICE. Shakespeare! The Queen—the Queen has asked for you,
And sent her woman twice. Will Shakespeare! Will!

SHAKESPEARE. At midnight then.

MRS. HATHAWAY *goes out.*

VOICE. Will Shakespeare!

SHAKESPEARE. Coming! Coming!

MARY [*in the doorway, followed by* MARLOWE].
Is Shakespeare—?

SHAKESPEARE. Oh, not now, not now, not now!

MARY. Are you mad to keep her waiting? She has favours up her sleeve. You are to write her a play for the summer revels. Quick now, ere the last act begins! Off with you! [SHAKESPEARE *goes out.*] Look how he drags away! What's come to the man to fling aside his luck?

MARLOWE. He has left it behind him.

MARY. Here's a proxy silver-tongue! Are you Mr. Marlowe?

MARLOWE. Are you Mistress Fitton?

MARY. So we've heard of each other!

MARLOWE. What have you heard of me?

MARY. That you were somebody's brother-in-art! What have you heard of me?

MARLOWE. That you were his sister-in-art.

MARY. A man's sister! I'd as soon be a cold pudding! What did he say of his sister, brother?

MARLOWE. That you brought him luck.

MARY. That he leaves behind him!

MARLOWE. Like the blind man's lucky sixpence that the Jew stole when he put a penny in his plate.

MARY. A Jew of Malta?

MARLOWE. What, do *you* read me? You?

A STAGE HAND [*in the passage*]. Last act, please! Last act! Last act!

MARY. I must go watch it.

MARLOWE. Don't you know it?

MARY. Oh, by heart! Yet I must sisterly watch it.

MARLOWE. Stay a little.

MARY. Till he comes? Then I shall miss all, for he'll keep me.

MARLOWE. Against your will?

MARY. No, with my Will.

MARLOWE. Is it he or his plays?

MARY. Not sure.

MARLOWE. If I were he I'd make you sure.

MARY. I wonder if you could! I wonder—how?

MARLOWE. Too long to tell you here, and—curtain's up!

MARY. Come to my house one lazy day and tell me!

MARLOWE. Hark! That's more noise than curtain!

HENSLOWE'S VOICE. Shakespeare! Shakespeare! [*Entering.*] Here's a calamity! Where's Shakespeare? He should be in the green-room! Why does he tuck away in this rat-hole when he's wanted? And what's to be done? Where in God's name is Shakespeare?

MARY. With the Queen.

MARLOWE. The curtain's up; he'll be here in a minute.

MARY. What's wrong?

HENSLOWE. Everything! Juliet! The clumsy beasts! They let him fall from the bier: they let him fall on his arm! Now he's moaning and wincing and swears he can't go on, though he has but to speak his death scene. I've bid them cut the afterwards.

MARLOWE. Broken?

HENSLOWE. I fear so.

MARY.   Let it be broken! Say he must go on!
                  What? Spoil the play? These baby-men!

HENSLOWE.   He will not.

MARLOWE. The understudy?

HENSLOWE. Playing Paris. Where's Shakespeare? What's to be done? The play's spoiled.

MARLOWE.   He'll break his heart.

MARY.   He shall not break his heart!
                  This is our play! Back to your Juliet-boy,
                  Strip off his wear and never heed his arm!
                  Bid them play on and bring me Juliet's robes!
                  I'll put them on and put on Juliet too.
                  Quick, Henslowe!

HENSLOWE.   What! a woman play on the stage?

MARY.   Ay, when the men fail! Quick! I say I'll do it!

SHAKESPEARE [*entering*].
                  Here still? You've heard?

MARY [*on the threshold*].   And heeded. Never stop me!
                  You shall have Juliet. You shall have your play.

              She and HENSLOWE *hurry out.*

MARLOWE. There goes a man's master! But does she know the part?

SHAKESPEARE.   She knows each line, she knows each word, she
breathed them
Into my heart long ere I wrote them down.

MARLOWE.   But to act! Can you trust her?

SHAKESPEARE.   She? Go and watch! I need not.

MARLOWE.   But is it in her? She's Julia not Juliet, not your
young Juliet, not your June morning—or is she?

SHAKESPEARE.   You talk! You talk! You talk! What do you
know of her?

MARLOWE.   Or you, old Will?

SHAKESPEARE.   I dream her.

MARLOWE.   Well, pleasant dreams!

SHAKESPEARE.   No more. I'm black awake.

MARLOWE.   What's wrong? Ill news?

SHAKESPEARE.   From Stratford. Yes, yes, yes, Kit! And it must
come now, just now, after ten dumb years!

MARLOWE.   Stratford? Whew! I'd forgotten your nettle-bed.
What does she want of you?

SHAKESPEARE.   Hark! Mary's on.

MARLOWE.   It's a voice like the drip of a honey-comb.

SHAKESPEARE.   Can she play Juliet, man? Can she play Juliet?
I think she can. Kit?

MARLOWE.   Ay?

SHAKESPEARE.   Oh, is there peace
Anywhere, Kit, in any, any world?

MARLOWE.   What is it, peace?

SHAKESPEARE.   It passeth understanding.
They round the sermon off on Sunday with it,
Laugh in their sleeves and send us parching
home.
This is a dew that dries ere Monday comes,
And oh, the heat of the seven days!

MARLOWE.   I like it!
The smell of dust, the shouting, and the glare
Of crowded noon in cities, and such nights
As this night, crowning labour. What is—peace?

STAGE HAND [*entering*]. Sir, sir, sir, will you come down, sir, says Mr. Henslowe. The end's near and the house half mad. We've not seen a night like this since—since *your* night, sir! Your first night, sir, your roaring Tamburlaine night! Never anything like it and I've seen many. Will you come, sirs?

SHAKESPEARE. You go, Marlowe!

STAGE HAND. There's nothing to fear, sir! It runs like clockwork. The lady died well, sir! Lord, who'd think she was a woman! There, there, it breaks out. Listen to 'em! Come, sir, come, come!

MARLOWE. We'll come! We'll come!

The man goes out.

SHAKESPEARE. Not I! Oh, if you love me, Marlowe, swear I'm ill, gone away, dead, what you please, but keep them away! I can stand no more.

MARLOWE. It's as she said—mad—mad—to fling your luck away.

SHAKESPEARE. A frost has touched me, Marlowe, my fruit's black. Help me now! Go, go! Say I'm gone, as I shall be when I've seen Mary—

MARLOWE. A back stairs? Now I understand.

SHAKESPEARE. Oh, stop your laughter! I'm to leave London in half an hour.

MARLOWE. Earnest? For long?

SHAKESPEARE. Little or long, what matter? I've missed the moment. Who has his moment twice?

MARLOWE. Shall you tell her why you go?

SHAKESPEARE. Mary? God forbid!

VOICES. Shakespeare! Call Shakespeare!

SHAKESPEARE. D'you hear them? Help me! Say I am gone!
Oh, go, go!
MARLOWE. Well, if you wish it!

> *He goes out leaving the door ajar. As* SHAKESPEARE
> *goes on speaking the murmurs and claps die away and the*
> *noises of the stage are heard, the shouts of the scene-shifters,*
> *directions being given, and so on. Finally there is silence.*

SHAKESPEARE.   Wish it? I wish it? Have you no more for me
Of comfort, Marlowe?
Oh, what a dumb and measureless gulf divides
Star from twin star, and friend from closest
    friend!
Women, they say, can bridge it when they will:
As seamen rope a ship with grappling irons
These spinners of strong cords invisible
Make fast and draw the drifting glory home
In the name of love. I know not. Better go!
I am not for this harbour—

> *There is a sound of hasty footsteps and*
> MARY FITTON *enters in Juliet's robes. She*
> *stands in the doorway, panting, exalted,*
> *with arms outstretched. The door swings*
> *to behind her, shutting out all sound.*

MARY.   Oh, I faced
The peacock of the world, the arch of eyes
That watched me love a god, the eyes, eyes, eyes,
That watched me die of love. Wake me again,
O soul that did inhabit me, O husband
Whose mind I uttered, to whose will I swayed,
Whose self of love I was! Wake me again
To die of love in earnest!

SHAKESPEARE.   Mary! Mary!

MARY.   I cannot ride this hurricane. I spin
Like a leaf in the air. Die down and let me lie
Close to the earth I am! O stir me not
With rosy breathings from the south, the south
Of sun and wine and peaks that flame to God
Suddenly in the dark! O wind, let be
And drive me not; for speech lies on my lips
Like a strange finger hushing back my soul
With words not mine, and thoughts not mine arise
Like marsh-flame dancing! As a leaf to a tree
Upblown, O wind that whirls me, I return.
Master and quickener, give me love indeed!

SHAKESPEARE.   These are the hands I never held till now:
These are the lips I never felt on mine:
This is the hour I dreamed of, many an hour:
This is the spirit awake. God in your sky,
Did your heart beat so on the seventh dawn?

MARY.   'Ware thunder!

SHAKESPEARE.   Sweet, He envies and is dumb,
Dumb as His dark. He was our audience.
Now to His blinding centrum home He hies,
Omnipotent drudge, to wind the clocks of Time
And tend His 'plaining universes all—
To us, to us, His empty theatre of night
Abandoning. But we too steal away;
For the play's done,
Lights out—all over—and here we stand alone,
Holding each other in a little room,
Like two souls in one grave. We are such lovers—

ANNE'S VOICE. As there's no room for in the human air
And green side of the grass—

SHAKESPEARE.   A voice!   A voice!

MARY.   No voice here!

SHAKESPEARE.   In my heart I heard it cry
Like a sick child waked suddenly at night.

[*Crying out*]

A child—a sick child!   Unlink your arms that
     hold me!

MARY.   Never till I choose!

SHAKESPEARE.   Put back your hair!   I am lost
Unless I lose all gain.   O moonless night,
In your hot darkness I have lost my way!
But kiss me, summer, once!   On London Bridge
At midnight—I'll be there!   Has the clock
     struck?

MARY.   Midnight long since.

SHAKESPEARE.   Oh, I am damned and lost
In hell for ever!

MARY.   Fool, dear fool, what harm?
If this be hell indeed, is not hell kind?
Is not hell lovely, if this love be hell?
Is not damnation sweet?

SHAKESPEARE.   God does not know
How sweet, how sweet!

MARY.   Were they not wise, those two
Whose same blood beats again in you and me,
That chose the desert and the fall and went
Exultant from their garden and their God?
Long shall the sworded angels stand at ease
And idly guard the undesired delight:
Long shall the grasses grow and tall the briars,
And bent the branches of the ancient trees:

And many a year the wilding flowers shall blaze
Under a lonely sun, and fruited sweets
Shall drop and rot, and feed the roots that feed,
And bud again and ripen: long and long
Silent the watchman-lark in heaven shall hang
High over Eden, e'er they come again
Those two, whose blood is our blood, and their love
Our love, our own, that no god gave us, ours,
The venture ours, the glory ours, the shame
A price worth paying, then, now, ever—

SHAKESPEARE.
                                Eve,
Eve, Eve, the snake has been with you! You draw,
You drink my soul as I your body—

MARY.
                                Kiss!

THE CURTAIN FALLS.

ACT III.

SCENE I.

[SHAKESPEARE'S *lodging. It is the plain but well-arranged room of a man of fair means and fine taste. The walls are panelled: on them hang a couple of unframed engravings, a painting, tapestry, and a map of the known world. There is a four-post bed with a coverlet and hangings of needlework, and on the window-sill a pot of early summer flowers. There is a chair or two of oak and a table littered with papers. SHAKESPEARE is sitting at it, a manuscript in his hand. On the arm of the chair lolls MARLOWE, one arm flung round SHAKESPEARE'S neck, reading over his shoulder.*]

SHAKESPEARE. Man, how you've worked! A whole act to my ten lines! You dice all day and dance all night and yet—how do you do it?

MARLOWE. Like it?

SHAKESPEARE. Like it? What a word for a word-master! Consider, Kit! When the sun rises like a battle song over the sea: when the wind's feet visibly race along the tree-tops of a ten-mile wood: when they shout "Amen!" in the Abbey, praying for the Queen on Armada Day: when the sky is a brass gong and the rain steel rods, and across all suddenly arch the seven colours of the promise—do I *like* these wonders when I stammer and weep, and know that God lives? Like, Marlowe!

MARLOWE. Yes, yes, old Will! But do you like the new act?

SHAKESPEARE. I like it, Kit! [*They look at each other and laugh.*]

MARLOWE. And now for your scene, ere I go.

SHAKESPEARE. My scene! I give you what I've done. Finish it alone, Kit, and take what it brings! I'm sucked dry.

MARLOWE. I've heard that before.

SHAKESPEARE. I wish I had never come to London.

MARLOWE. Henslowe's back. Seen him?

SHAKESPEARE. I've seen no-one. Did the tour go well?

MARLOWE. He says so. He left them at Stratford. Well, I must go.

SHAKESPEARE. Where? To Mary?

MARLOWE. Why should I go to your Mary?

SHAKESPEARE. Because I've asked you to, often enough. Why else? You've grown to be friends. You could help me if you would.

MARLOWE. Never step between a man and a woman!

SHAKESPEARE. But you're our friend! And they say you know women.

MARLOWE. They say many things. They say we're rivals, Will— that I shall end by having you hissed.

SHAKESPEARE. Let them say! But have you seen Mary? When did you last see Mary?

MARLOWE. I forget. Saturday.

SHAKESPEARE. Did you speak of me, Kit? Kit, does she speak of me?

MARLOWE. If you must have it—seldom. New songs, new books, new music—of plays and players and the Queen's tantrums—not of you.

SHAKESPEARE. I have not seen her three days.

MARLOWE. Why, go then and see her!

SHAKESPEARE. She has company. She is waiting on the Queen. She gives me a smile and a white cool finger-tip, and—"Farewell, Mr. Shakespeare!" Yet a month ago, ay and less than a month—! Did you give her my message? What did she say?

MARLOWE. She laughed and says you dream. She never liked you better.

SHAKESPEARE. Did she say that?

MARLOWE. She says you cool to her, not she to you.

SHAKESPEARE. Did she say that?

MARLOWE. Swore it, with tears in her eyes.

SHAKESPEARE. Is it so? I wish it were so. Well, you're my good friend, Marlowe!

MARLOWE. Oh, leave that!

SHAKESPEARE. Kit, do you blame me so much?

MARLOWE. Why should I blame you?

SHAKESPEARE. That I'm here and not in Warwickshire.

MARLOWE. I throw no stones. Why? Have you heard aught?

SHAKESPEARE. No, nor dared ask—nor dared ask, Marlowe. The boy's dead. I know it. But I will not hear it. Marlowe, Marlowe, Marlowe, do you judge me?

MARLOWE. Ay, that putting your hand to the plough you look back. Would I comb out my conscience daily as a woman combs out her hair? I do what I choose, though it damn me! Blame you? The round world has not such another Mary—or so, had I your eyes, I should hold. For this prize, if I loved her, I would pay away all I had.

SHAKESPEARE. Honour, Kit?

MARLOWE. Honour, Will!

SHAKESPEARE. Faith and conscience and an only son?

MARLOWE. It's my own life. What are children to me?

SHAKESPEARE. Well, I have paid.

MARLOWE. But you grudge—you grudge! Look at you! If you go to her with those eyes it's little wonder that she tires of you.

SHAKESPEARE. Tires? Who says that she tires? Who says it?

MARLOWE. Not I, old Will! Not I! Why, Shakespeare?

SHAKESPEARE [shaken]. I can't sleep, Kit! I can't write. What has come to me? I think I go mad. [He starts.] Was that the boy on the stairs? I sent him to her. I wrote. I have waited her will long enough. She shall see me to-night. I'll know what it means. She plays with me, Kit. Are you going?

MARLOWE. I shall scarce reach Deptford ere dark.

SHAKESPEARE. How long do you lodge in Deptford?

MARLOWE. All summer.

HENSLOWE [*pounding at the door*]. Who's at home? Who's at home?

MARLOWE. That's Henslowe.

SHAKESPEARE. Why does the boy stay so long?

HENSLOWE [*in the doorway*]. Gentlemen, the traveller returns! For the last time, I tell you! My bones grow too old for barnstorming. Do you go as I come, Kit? Thank you for nothing!

MARLOWE. Be civil, Henslowe! 'The Curtain' 's on its knees to me for my next play.

HENSLOWE. Pooh! This man can serve my turn.

MARLOWE. You see, they'll make rivals of us, Will, before they've done. I'll see you soon again. [*He goes out.*]

HENSLOWE. Well, what's the news?

SHAKESPEARE. I sit at home. You roam England. You can do the talking. How did the tour go?

HENSLOWE. You're thin, man! What's the matter? Success doesn't suit you?

SHAKESPEARE. How did the tour go?

HENSLOWE. By way of Oxford, Warwick, Kenilworth—

SHAKESPEARE. I said "how" not "where."

HENSLOWE. —and Leamington and Stratford. We played 'Romeo' every other night—and to full houses, my son! I've a pocketful of money for you. They liked you everywhere. As for your townsfolk, they went mad. You can safely go home, boy! You'll find Sir Thomas in the front row, splitting his gloves. He'll ask you to dinner.

SHAKESPEARE. Were you there long?

HENSLOWE. Two nights.

SHAKESPEARE. Did you see—anyone?

HENSLOWE. Why not say—

SHAKESPEARE. I say, did you pass my house?

HENSLOWE. I had forgot the way.

SHAKESPEARE.   As I have, Henslowe!

HENSLOWE. Should I have sought her?

SHAKESPEARE.   No.

HENSLOWE.   Yet I did see her.
Making for London, not a week ago,
Alone on horseback, sudden the long grey road
Grew friendly, like a stranger in a dream
Nodding "I know you!" and behold, a love
Long dead, that smiles and says, "I never died!"
Then in the turn of the lane I saw your thatch.
Summer not winter, else was all unchanged.
Still in the dream I left my horse to graze,
And let ten years slip from me at your gate.

SHAKESPEARE. Is it ten years?

HENSLOWE.   The little garden lay
Enchanted in the Sunday sloth of noon:
In th' aspen tree the wind hung, fast asleep,
Yet the air danced a foot above the flowers
And gnats danced in it. I saw a poppy-head
Spilling great petals, noiseless, one by one:
I heard the honeysuckle breathe—sweet, sweet:
The briar was sweeter—a long hedge, pink-
    starred—

SHAKESPEARE. I know.

HENSLOWE.   There was a bush of lavender,
And roses, and a bee in every rose,

Drowning the lark that fluted, fields away,
Up in the marvel blue.

SHAKESPEARE.   Did you go in?

HENSLOWE. Why, scarce I dared, for as I latched the gate
The wind stirred drowsily, and "Hush!" it said,
And slept again; but all the garden waked
Upon the sound. I swear, as I play Prologue,
It watched me, waiting. Down the path I crept,
Tip-toe, and reached the window, and looked in.

SHAKESPEARE. You saw—?

HENSLOWE.   I saw her; though the place was
                              gloom
After the sunshine; but I saw her—

SHAKESPEARE.   Changed?

HENSLOWE. I knew her.

SHAKESPEARE.   Who was with her?

HENSLOWE.   She was alone,
Beside the hearth unkindled, sitting alone.
A child's chair was beside her, but no child.
Her hands were sleepless, and beneath her breath
She tuned a thread of song—your song of
     'Willow.'
But when I tapped upon the window-pane,
Oh, how she turned, and how leaped up! Her
     face
Glowed white as iron new lifted from the forge:
Her hair fled out behind her in one flame
As to the door she ran, with little cries
Scarce human, tearing at the bolt, the key,
And flung it crashing back: ran out, wide-armed,
Calling your name: then—saw me, and stood
     still,

So still you'd think she died there, standing up,
As a sapling will in frost, so desolate
She stood, with summer round her, staring—

SHAKESPEARE.   Well?

HENSLOWE. I asked her, did she know me? Yes, she said,
And would I rest and eat? So much she said
To the lawn behind me—oh, to the hollyhock
Stiff at my elbow—to a something—nothing—
But not to me. I could not eat her food.
I told her so. She nodded. Oh, she knows
How thoughts run in a man. No fool, no fool!
I spoke of you. She listened.

SHAKESPEARE.   Questioned you?

HENSLOWE. Never a question.

SHAKESPEARE.   She said nothing?

HENSLOWE.   Nothing.

SHAKESPEARE. Not like her.

HENSLOWE.   But her eyes spoke, as I came
By way of London, Juliet, 'The Rose,'
And the Queen's great favour ("And why not?"
    they said)
Again to silence; so, as I turned to go
I asked her—"Any greeting?" Then she said,
Lifting her chin as if she sped her words
Far, far, like pigeons flung upon the air,
And soft her voice as bird-wings—then she said,
"Tell him the woods are green at Shottery,
Fuller of flowers than any wood in the world."
"What else?" said I. She said—"The wind
    still blows
Fresh between park and river. Tell him that!"
Said I—"No message, letter?" Then she said,

                Twisting her hands—"Tell him the days are long.

                Tell him—" and suddenly ceased. Then, with good-bye

                Pleasantly spoken, and another look

                At some wraith standing by me, not at me,

                Went back into the house and shut the door.

SHAKESPEARE.   Ay, shut the door, Henslowe; for had she been this she

                Ten years ago and I this other I—

                Well, I have friends to love! Heard Marlowe's news?

                He's three-part through Leander! Oh, this Marlowe!

                I mine for coal but he digs diamonds.

HENSLOWE.   Yet fill your scuttle lest the world grow chill! Is the new play done?

SHAKESPEARE. No.

HENSLOWE. Much written?

SHAKESPEARE. Not a line.

HENSLOWE. Are you mad? We're contracted. What shall I say to the Queen?

SHAKESPEARE. What you please.

HENSLOWE. Are you well?

SHAKESPEARE. Well enough.

HENSLOWE. Ill enough, I think.

SHAKESPEARE.   Write your own plays—bid Marlowe, any man

                That writes as nettles grow or rain comes down!

                I am not born to it. I write not so.

                Romeo and Juliet—I am dead of them!

                The pay's too small, good clappers! These ghosts need blood

To make 'em plump and lively and they know it,
And seek their altar. Threads and floating wisps
Of being, how they fasten like a cloud
Of gnats upon me, not to be shoo'd off
Unsatisfied—and they drink deep, drink deep;
For like a pelican these motes I feed,
And with old griefs' remembrance and old joys'
Sharper remembrance daily scourge myself,
And still they crowd to suck my scars and live.

HENSLOWE. Now, now, now—do I ask another 'Juliet' of you?
God forbid! A fine play, your 'Juliet,' but—

SHAKESPEARE. Now come the "buts."

HENSLOWE. Man, we must live! Can we fill the theatre on love
and longing, and high words? Ay, when Marlowe does it to the
sound of trumpets. But you—you're not Marlowe. You know too
much. Your gods are too much men and women. Who'll pay
sixpence for a heart-ache? and in advance too! Give us but two
more 'Romeo and Juliet's and you may be a great poet, but we close
down. Another tragedy? No, no, no, we don't ask that of you!
We want light stuff, easy stuff. Oh, who knows as well as you what's
wanted? It's a court play, my man! The French Embassy's to be
there and the two Counts from Italy, and always Essex and his
gang, and you know *their* fancy. Get down to it now, there's a good
lad! Oh, you can do it in your sleep! Lovers and lasses, and
quarrels and kisses, like the two halves of a sandwich! But court
lovers, you know, that talk verse—and between them a green cress
of country folk and country song, daffodils and valentines, and brown
bowls of ale season all with a pepper of wit—and there's your
sandwich, there's your play, as the Queen likes it, as we all like it!

SHAKESPEARE.   Ay, as you like it! There's your title pat!
But I'll not serve you. I'm to live, not write.
Tell that to the Queen!

A boy enters whistling and stops as he sees SHAKESPEARE.

Well, Hugh, what answer?

BOY.   None, sir!

SHAKESPEARE. What? No answer?

HENSLOWE. See here, Will! If you do not write me this play you have thrice promised, I'll to the Queen—sick or mad I'll to the Queen this very day for your physic—and so I warn you.

SHAKESPEARE [*to the boy*]. Did you see—?

BOY. The maid, sir!

HENSLOWE. I'll not see 'The Rose' in ruins for a mad—

SHAKESPEARE [*to the boy*]. But what did I bid you?

BOY. Wait on the doorstep till Mistress Fitton came out, though I waited all night. But indeed, sir, she's gone; for I saw her, though she did not see me.

HENSLOWE. Oh, the Fitton! Now I see light through the wood!

SHAKESPEARE. What's that you say?

HENSLOWE. I say that the Queen shall know where the blame lies.

SHAKESPEARE. You lie. *I* heard you. *I* saw you twist your lips round a white name.

HENSLOWE. Will! Will! Will!

SHAKESPEARE. Did you not?

HENSLOWE. Why, Will, you have friends, though you fray 'em to the parting of endurance.

SHAKESPEARE. What's this?

HENSLOWE. I say you have friends that see what they see, and are sorry.

SHAKESPEARE. Yes, I am blessed in one man and woman who do not use me as a beast to be milked dry. I have Marlowe and—

HENSLOWE. Marlowe? And I said, God forgive me, that you knew men and women! Marlowe!

SHAKESPEARE. You speak of my friend.

HENSLOWE. Ay, Jonathan—of David, the singer, of him that took Bathsheba, all men know how. [SHAKESPEARE *makes a threatening movement.*] No, no, Will! I am too old a man to give and take with you—too old a man and too old a friend.

SHAKESPEARE. So you're to lie and I'm to listen because you're an old man!

HENSLOWE. Lie? Ask any in the town. I'm but a day returned and already I've heard the talk. Why, man, they make songs of it in the street!

SHAKESPEARE. It? It? It?

HENSLOWE. Boy?

BOY. Here, sir?

HENSLOWE. What was that song you whistled as you came up the stairs?

BOY. 'Weathercock,' sir?

HENSLOWE. That's it!

BOY. Lord, sir, I know but the one verse I heard a drayman sing.

HENSLOWE. How does it go?

BOY. It goes—[*singing*].

> Two birds settle on a weathercock—
> How's the wind to-day—O?
> One shall nest and one shall knock—
> How's the wind to-day—O?
> Turn about and turn about,
> Kit pops in as Will pops out!
> Winds that whistle round the weathercock,
> Who's her love to-day—O?

It's a good tune, sir!

HENSLOWE. Eh, Will? A good tune! A rousing tune!

SHAKESPEARE [*softly*]. "For this prize, if I loved her, I would pay all I had! I do what I choose though it damn me!"

BOY. May I go, sir?

Joanne Desert

SHAKESPEARE. Go, go!

BOY. And my pay, sir? Indeed, I'd have stopped the lady if I could. But she made as if she were not herself, and rode out of the yard. But I knew her, for all her riding-coat and breeches.

HENSLOWE. What's all this?

SHAKESPEARE [*to the boy*]. You're dreaming—

BOY. No, sir, there was your ring on her finger—

SHAKESPEARE. Be still! Take this and forget your dreams! [*He gives him money.*] Henslowe, farewell! If you've lied to me I'll pay you for it, and if you've spoken truth to me I'll pay you for it no less.

HENSLOWE. Pay? I want no pay. I want the play that the Queen ordered, and will have in the end, mark that! You have not yet served the Queen.

SHAKESPEARE. Boy! Hugh!

BOY. Sir?

SHAKESPEARE. Which way did she ride?

BOY. Am I asleep or awake, sir?

SHAKESPEARE. Which way did she ride?

BOY. Across the bridge, sir, as I dreamt it, along the Deptford road.

SHAKESPEARE. Marlowe! The Deptford road! The Deptford road! [*He rushes out.*]

BOY [*showing his money*]. Dreaming pays, sir! It's gold.

HENSLOWE. Boy, boy! Never trust a man! Never kiss a woman! Work all day and sleep all night! Love yourself and never ask God for the moon! So you may live to be old. This business grows beyond me. I'll to the Queen.

> *He trots out, shaking his head. The boy skips after him, whistling his tune.*

THE CURTAIN FALLS.

ACT III.

Scene II.

A private room at an inn late at night. Through the door in the right wall is seen the outer public room, with men sitting drinking. There is a window at the back, set so low in the wall that, above the window-sill, the heads of summer flowers glisten in the moonlight. On the left wall is the hearth and between it and the window a low bed. In the centre is a table with candle, glasses and mugs, and two or three men sitting round it drinking. Marlowe stands with his back to the window, one foot on a chair, shouting out a song as the curtain rises.

Marlowe [*singing*].

> If Luck and I should meet
> I'll catch her to me crying,
> 'To trip with you were sweet,
> Have done with your denying!'
> Hey, lass! Ho, lass!
> Heel and toe, lass!
> Who'll have a dance with me?

All Together.
> Hey, Luck! Ho, Luck!
> Ne'er say no, Luck!
> I'll have a dance with thee!

A Man [*hammering the table*]. Again! Again!

Landlord [*at the door*]. Sir, sir, there's without a young gentleman hot with riding—

Marlowe. Does the hot young gentleman give no name?

LANDLORD. Why yes, sir, Archer, Francis Archer! He said you would know him.

MARLOWE. I knew an Archer, but he died in Flanders.

LANDLORD. He may well come from Flanders, sir, for he's muddy.

MARLOWE. Are Flanders' graves so shallow? Tell him if he's alive I don't know him, and if he's dead I won't know him, and so either way let him go where he belongs.

The LANDLORD *goes out.*

THE MAN. What, Kit! send him to hell with a dry throat?

MARLOWE. And all impostors with him!

THE MAN. But what if it were a true ghost? Have a heart! You'll be one yourself some day, and watch old friends run away from you when you come to haunt them in pure good fellowship.

LANDLORD [*at the door*]. Sir, he says indeed he knows you. His business is private.

MARLOWE. Well, let him come in. No, friends, sit still! If he's the death he pretends we'll face him together as the song teaches.

[*Singing.*] When Death at last arrives,
　　　　　I'll greet him with a chuckle,
　　　　　I'll ask him how he thrives
　　　　　And press his bony knuckle,
　　　　　　　With—Ho, boy! Hey, boy!
　　　　　　　Come this way, boy!
　　　　　Who'll have a drink with me?

MARY'S VOICE [*on the stairs*].
　　　　　　　Hey, Sir! Ho, Sir!
　　　　　　　No, no, no, Sir!
　　　　　Why should he drink with thee?
ALL TOGETHER. 　　Hey, Death! Ho, Death!
　　　　　　　Let me go, Death!
　　　　　I'll never drink with thee!

MARLOWE. What voice is that?

MARY *stands in the doorway. She is dressed as a boy, with cloak, riding boots, and slouch cap.*

MARY [*singing*]. If Love should pass me by,
> I'll follow till I find him,
> And when I hear him sigh,
> I'll tear the veils that blind him.
>> Up, man! Dance, man!
>> Take your chance, man!
> Who'll get a kiss from me?

ALL TOGETHER.   Hey, Love! Ho, Love!
> None shall know, Love!
>> Keep but a kiss for me!   [*They clap.*]

THE MAN [*to* MARLOWE]. Ghost of a nightingale! D'you know him?

MARLOWE. I think I do. [*To* MARY, *aside.*] What April freak is this?

THE MAN [*with a glass*]. Spirits to spirit, young sir! Have a drink?

MARY. I should choke, sir! We drink nectar in my country.

THE MAN. Where's that, ghost?

MARY. Oh, somewhere on the soft side of heaven where the poppies grow.

THE MAN. He swore you were dead and buried.

MARY. And so I was. But there's a witch in London so sighs for him and so cries for him, that in the end she whistled me out of my gravity and sent me here to fetch him home to her.

THE MAN. Her name, transparency, her name?

MARY. Why, sir, I rode in such haste that my memory could not keep up with me. It'll not be here this half hour.

MARLOWE. Landlord, pour ale for a dozen, and these friends will drink to her, name or no name—in the next room.

THE MAN. Kit, you're a man of tact! I'm a man of tact. We're all men of tact!

> Ho, boys! Hey, boys!
> Come this way, boys!
> Who'll have a drink with me?

The door closes on them.

MARY. Well, did you ever see a better boy? My hair was the only trouble.

MARLOWE. Madcap! What does this mean?

MARY. What I said! [*singing*].

> Moth, where are you flown?
> To burn in a flame!
> Moth, I lie alone—

You've not been near me these four days.

MARLOWE. Uneasy days—I could not.

MARY. Are you burned, moth? Are the poor wings a frizzle?

MARLOWE. Not mine, dear candle, but a king of moths,
But a great hawk-moth, velvet as the night
He beats with twilight wings, he, he is singed,
Fallen to earth and pitiful.

MARY. Oh, Shakespeare!
My dear, I've run away because I hate
The smell of burning.

He was to come to me to-night to tell me his tragedies and his comedies and—oh, I yawn! And I played her so well too at the first—

MARLOWE. Who?

MARY. The cool nymph under Tiber stairs—what's her name?— Egeria. Am I your Egeria, Marlowe?

MARLOWE. Something less slippery.

MARY. Oh, she was fun to play—first to please the Queen and

then to please myself. For I was caught, you know. It's something
to be hung among the stars, something to say—"I was his Juliet!"

MARLOWE. What, you—you Comedy-Kate?

MARY.   Why, I'm a woman! that is—fifty women!
          While he played Romeo to my Juliet
          I could be anything he chose. O Kit!
          I sucked his great soul out. You never lit the
               blaze
          I was for half an hour: then—out I went!

MARLOWE.   He stoops o'er the embers yet.

MARY.   But ashes fanned
          Fly from their centre, lighter than a kiss,
          And settle—where they please! [*She kisses
               him.*]

D'you love me?

MARLOWE. More than I wish.

MARY. Would you be cured?

MARLOWE. Not possible.

MARY [*singing*].   Go to church, sweetheart,
               A flower in your coat!
               Your wedding bells shall prove
          The death of love! The death of love!
               Ding-dong! Ding-dong!
               The death of love!

Or so Will says.

MARLOWE. He should know.

MARY. What's that?

MARLOWE. Nothing.

MARY. He's married?

MARLOWE. I do not tell you so.

MARY. Married! He shall pay me. Married! I guessed it—but
he shall pay me. A country girl?

MARLOWE. If you must know! He has not seen her these ten
years. She sent for him the night of 'Juliet.'

MARY.　　　　　　Why now all's plain.

So she's the canker that hath drooped our
rose!

If I had loved him—I do not love him, Marlowe—
This would have fanned a flame. Well, we're
all cheats!

But now I cheat with better conscience. Married!
Lord, I could laugh! He must not know I know it.

MARLOWE. I shan't boast I told you. O Mary, when I first came
to you, it was he sent me. He came like a child and asked me to
see you, to say what good of him I could,

Because I was his friend. And now, see, see,
How I have friended him!

MARY.　　　　　　　　　　　　I love you for it.

He shall not know. Why talk of him? Forget
him?

MARLOWE.　　　　Can you?

MARY.　　　　　Why, that I cannot makes me mad—

MARLOWE.　　　　　　　　　　　Forget him?

As soon forget myself! I am his courage,
His worldly wisdom—Mary, I think I am
The youth he lost in Stratford. Yet we're one
age,
And now we write one play. If I died of a
sudden,
It seems he'd breathe me as I left my body,
And I should live in him as sunshine lies
Forgotten in a forest, and be found
In slants and pools and patterns, golden still
In all he writes.

MARY. O dull Kit! have I adventured here to hear you talk
of dying?

MARLOWE. You borrowed Archer's name.

MARY. I wanted one that would startle you out to me, and you
told me the tale of him once, how young he died.

MARLOWE. And how unwilling! You've set him running in my
head like a spider in a skull,

> Spinning across the hollows of mine eyes
> A web of dusty thought. Sweet, brush him off!
> Death's a vile dreg in this intoxicant,
> This liquor of the gods, this seven-hued life.
> Sometimes I pinch myself, say—"Can you die?
> Is it possible? Will you be winter-nipped
> One day like other flies?" I'm glad you came.
> Stay with me, stay, till the last minute of life!
> Let the court go, the world go, stay with me!

MARY [*her arms round him*].

> So—quiet till the dawn comes, quiet! Hark!
> Who called? Did you hear it?

MARLOWE.   Birds in the ivy.
MARY.   No.

> Twice in the road I stopped and turned about
> Because I heard my name called. There was
>   nothing;
> Yet I had heard it—Mary—Mary—Mary!

MARLOWE. You heard your own heart pound from riding.
MARY.   Again!

> Open the window! [MARLOWE *rises and goes to
>   the window.*]
>   Do you see anything?

MARLOWE. All's sinister. The moon fled out of the sky
> Long since, and the black trees of midnight quake.

MARY.   And the wind! What a wind! It tugs at the
            window-frame
            Like jealousy, mad to break in and part us.
            Could you be jealous?

MARLOWE.   If I were a fool
            I'd let you guess it.

MARY.   Wise, you're wise, but—jealous?
            Too many men in the world! I'd lift no finger
            To beckon back the fool that tired of me,
            Would you? But he, he glooms and says no
                word,
            But follows with his eyes when e'er I stir.
            I hate those asking eyes. Look thus at me
            But once and—ended, Marlowe! I'll not give
            But when I choose.   [*He sits beside her.*]

MARLOWE.   But when *I* choose.

            *Behind them the blur of the window is
            darkened.*

MARY [*in his arms*].   Why yes!
            Had he your key-word—! Sometimes I like
                him yet,
            When anger comes in a white lightning flash,
            Then he's the man of men still, then with shut
                eyes
            I think him you and shiver and I like him,
            Held roughly in his arms, thinking of you.
            The Warwick burr is like an afterwards
            Of thunder when he's angry, in his speech.

MARLOWE.   What does he say?

MARY.   He says he is not jealous!
            He would not wrong me so, nor wrong himself.

Then the sky lightens and we kiss—or kiss not!
Who cares?
Then in come you. It's well he thinks you his
In friendship—

MARLOWE.   So I was.

     SHAKESPEARE *swings himself noiselessly
over the sill.*

MARY.   And so you are,
And have all things in common as friends should.
Eh, friend?
Oh, stir not! Frowning? If you were a fool—
(How did it run?) you'd let me guess you—
    jealous!
But you're no fool.

MARLOWE.   Let's have no more! You know
I loved—I love the man.

MARY.   Why, so do I.

MARLOWE. You shall not!

MARY.   Then I will not. Not to-night.

SHAKESPEARE [*standing by the window*].
Why not to-night, my lover and my friend?

    *He comes down into the room as they start
up.*

Will you not give me wine and welcome me?
Sit down, sit down—we three have much to say!
But tell me first, what does that hand of yours
Upon her neck, as there were custom in it?
Part! Part, I say! Part! lest I couple you
Once and for all!

MARY.   He's armed!

MARLOWE.   He shall not touch you!

SHAKESPEARE. You, Marlowe! You!

MARLOWE.   Stand out of her way!

SHAKESPEARE   You! You!

MARLOWE. Why then—

> MARLOWE *darts at* SHAKESPEARE *and is thrown off. He staggers against the table, knocking over the candle. As he strikes the second time his arm is knocked up, striking his own forehead. He falls across the bed. There is an instant's pause, then* SHAKE-SPEARE *rushes to him, slipping an arm under his shoulder.*

MARY.   Dead? Is he dead? Oh, what an end!

I never saw a dead man. Will—to me!

SHAKESPEARE. ,Get help!

MARY.   I dare not.

MARLOWE.   Oh!

SHAKESPEARE.   What is it?

MARLOWE.   Oh!

My life, my lovely life, and cast away
Untasted, wasted—
Death, let me go!   [*He dies.*]

MARY.   What now? Rouse up! Delay
Is dangerous. Wake! Wake! What shall we do?

SHAKESPEARE. O trumpet of the angels lent to a boy,
Could I not spare you for the golden blast,
For the great sound's sake? What have I done?

ANNE'S VOICE.   Ah! Done
The thing you would not do—

MARY.   Rouse! Rouse yourself!
What now?

ANNE'S VOICE.   Remember—

SHAKESPEARE.   Hark! A sigh!

MARY.   The wind
Keening the night—

SHAKESPEARE.   A sound of weeping—

MARY.   Rain.
Is this a time for visions? White-cheeked day
Stares through the pane. Each minute is an eye
Opening upon us. What shall we do now?

SHAKESPEARE. Weep, clamorous harlot! We have given him
         death,
And shall we dock his rights of death, his peace
Upon his bed, his sun of hair smoothed, hands
Crossed decently by me, his friend? Close you
His eyes with kisses, lest I kill you too!
Give him his due, I say! his woman's tears!
You were his woman—oh, deny it not!
You were his woman. Pay him what you owe!

MARY. What? Do you glove my clean hand with your
         stain,
Red fingers? Soft! This is your kill, not mine!
My free soul is not sticky with your sins.
You pinch your lips? *You* singe me with your
         tongue?
Your country lilac that you left for me
Taught you strange names for a woman. Harlot?
         I?
Sweep your own stable, trickster, married man!
Lie, cheat, break faith, until you end a man
That bettered you as roses better weeds—

SHAKESPEARE.
MARY.

That is well known.

              —and now you'll stare and weep
Until the watch comes and the Queen hears all.
Then—ends all!
And I caught with you! She's a devil of ice
Since Leicester died. No man or woman stirs
    her;
But she must have her toys! London's her
    doll's house,
Its marts, its theatres. This death was half
    her pride,
And you the other. Was I not set to mould you?
What will she do to me now her doll's broken,
Broken in my hand? I fear her, oh, I fear her,
The green eyes of her justice and her smile.
Will, if you love me—you who have had my lips,
And more, and more, and shall have all again,
All that you choose, and gladly given—awake!
Fly while there's time to save yourself and me!
Look not on him—he's blind—he cannot speak,
Nor stretch a hand to stay you—he's cold
    nothing!
But we, we live! Here on my throat, here, here,
(Give me your fingers!) feel the hot pulse live!
Yet I'll die sooner than be pent. You know me!
Must I lie still for ever at his side
Because you will not rouse yourself?

SHAKESPEARE

                      Who speaks?
O vanished dew, O summer sweetness gone,
O perfume staled in a night, that yesterday
Was fresh as morning roses—do you live?
Are you still Mary? O my shining lamp

Of love put out, how dark the world has grown!
Did you want him so? Did it come on you
    suddenly,
And shake you from your north—

MARY.   The dawn! the dawn!

SHAKESPEARE.   Or did you never love me—where do you
    point?

MARY.   To save ourselves comes first!

SHAKESPEARE.   To answer me!

MARY.   Fool! Fool! Will you hang? Let go, fool!

SHAKESPEARE.   Answer me!

MARY.   Will, for the love of living—

SHAKESPEARE.   Answer me!

MARY.   I never loved you. Are you answered?

ANNE'S VOICE.   Oh—
For a month—in the spring—

SHAKESPEARE.   Is it a month ago?
The trees are not yet metalled with the dust
Of summer, that were greening when we two—

MARY.   Oh, peace!

SHAKESPEARE.   —in a night of spring—

MARY.   Ah, was it love?

SHAKESPEARE.   Remember, Beauty, when you came to me,
As came the beggar to Cophetua,
As queens came conquered to the Macedon,
As Cressid came by night to Diomed,
As night comes queenly to the bed of day
Emmantled in her hair, so you to me,
Juliet, and all your night of hair was mine
To curtain me and you—

MARY.   Forgotten, forgotten—

SHAKESPEARE.   That night you loved me—

ANNE'S VOICE.   I was drunk with dreams
That night.

SHAKESPEARE.   That night of victory you loved me!
I have my witnesses. O watching stars—

MARY.   The eyes, the eyes, the arch of eyes!

SHAKESPEARE.   —speak for me!
Once was a taper that outshone you all,
It burned so bright. Oh, how you winked and
     pried!
I saw you through the tatters of the dark
And mocked you in my hour. Yet speak for me,
Eternal lights, for now my candle's blown
Past envy! But she loved me then!

MARY.   I know not.

SHAKESPEARE.   Though god and devil deny—you loved me then!

MARY.   But was it love?
I could have loved if you had taught me loving.
Something I sought and found not; so I turned
From searching. I have clean forgotten now
That ever I sought—and so live merrily—
And so will live! Why wreck myself for you?

SHAKESPEARE.   O heart's desire, and eyes', desire of hands,
Self of myself, have pity!

MARY.   What had you?
If I had borne you children (but I was wise,
Knowing my man, as men have taught me
     men)
What name had you to give them, to give me?
No, no, I wrong you, for you christened me
But now, first having slain him who had struck
The rankness from your mouth.

SHAKESPEARE.   What I have done—

MARY.
SHAKESPEARE.
ANNE'S VOICE.

Lied, lied to me!
           —and if I did—
                   To hold you!
I couldn't lose you. I was mad with pain.

MARY.
SHAKESPEARE.

Tricked me—
          To hold—listen to me—to hold you!
Lest I should lose you. I was mad with pain.

MARY.
SHAKESPEARE.

Are you so womanish that a breath of pain—
A breath! God, listen! A breath, a summer
     breath!

MARY.
SHAKESPEARE.

—could blow away your honour?
                  Once it was mine.
I laid it up with you. Where is it now?
I'm stripped of honour like an oak in June
Whose leaves a curse of caterpillars eat,
That stands a mockery to flowers and men,
With naked arms praying the lightning down.

ANNE'S VOICE.
SHAKESPEARE.
ANNE'S VOICE.
SHAKESPEARE.

At Shottery the woods are green—
                My God!
And full of flowers—
           Let be, let be! My honour?
I bought it with a woman—not like you,
A faithless-faithful woman—not like you;
But weak as I'm weak, loving as I love,
God help her! not like you—no black-eyed
     Spain
Whose cheeks hang out their red to match the red
When bull meets man—no luxury that wears
A lover like new clothes, and all the while
Eyes other women's fashions; but a woman
That should have loved me less, poor fool, and
     less—

MARY. You should have loved me less, my fool, and less!

SHAKESPEARE. Yet from this folly all the music springs
That is in the world, and all my hopes that ranged
Lark-high in heaven! Yet murder comes of it.
Look where he lies! He was true friend to me,
And I to him, until you came, you came.

MARY. I came and I can go.

SHAKESPEARE. Mary! [*There is a clatter of hoofs.*]

MARY. D'you hear?
Horses! What do they seek? You, Marlowe,
me?

SHAKESPEARE. This they call conscience.

MARY. Take your hand away!
I'll slip through yet; nor shall you follow me;
You had your chance. Listen! A boy was here;
One Francis Archer. Say it after me—
No woman, but a boy, a stranger to you!

SHAKESPEARE. Strange to me, Mary.

There is a sound of voices in the yard.

MARY. If you hold me now
I'll scream and swear you stabbed him as he slept,
They're drinking still. [*She opens the door.*]

VOICES [*in the outer room*].
Hey, boy! Ho, boy!
Heel and toe, boy!
Who'll have a drink with me?

MARY. If you should get away,
Send me no message, come not near me! Now!

She slips into the room. SHAKESPEARE
stands at the half open door watching.

A MAN. Sing another verse!

ANOTHER. There's the boy back. Make him sing it!

MARY. I'm to fetch more wine first.

THE MAN. Sing another verse!

ANOTHER.   If Love and I should meet,
                    I'll catch her to me—

ANOTHER. Luck, you fool, not love!

ANOTHER. Where's the difference? If you're in love you're in luck.

ANOTHER. Here, stop the boy!

MARY. Let me pass, gentlemen!

THE MAN. Sing another verse!

ANOTHER.   If Love and I—

ANOTHER. Shut up now and let the kid sing it!

MARY. Why yes, if you'll let me pass afterwards, sir, like love in the song.

THE MAN. Sing another verse! Sing twenty other verses!

MARY [*singing*].   If Love should pass me by,
                    I'll follow till I find him,
                  And when I hear him cry,
                    I'll tear the veils that blind him!

THE MAN. Now then, chorus!

ALL TOGETHER.   Hey, Love! Ho, Love!
                    None shall know, Love!
                  Keep but a kiss for me!

                    MARY *disappears in the crowd. The door
                    swings to as* SHAKESPEARE *turns back into
                    the room.*

SHAKESPEARE.   Marlowe! Marlowe!
                She is gone, Marlowe, that was a fume of wine
                Between us. Marlowe, Marlowe, speak to me!
                Never a sound. We have seen many a dawn

Creep like a house-wife on the drunken night,
And tumble him from heaven with work-day hand
And bird-shrill railing; but such a waking up
As this we never knew. Sorry and cold
I look on you. Kit, Kit, this mark of the knife
Is the first blot I ever saw in you,
The first ill-writing. Kit, for your own sake,
You should have wronged a stranger, not your
    friend;
For like a looking-glass my heart still served you
To see yourself, and when you struck at me,
You struck yourself, and broke this mirror too.
    A knock.
Mary? Is it Mary? Lie you quiet, Marlowe!
We will not let her in.

HENSLOWE.   Within, who's within there?
SHAKESPEARE.   Two dead men.
HENSLOWE.   Is it Marlowe?
Is Shakespeare there?
SHAKESPEARE.   Come in, come in, come in!
    HENSLOWE *comes in hurriedly. He leaves
    the door half open behind him.*
VOICES [*singing*].   Ho, boy! Hey, boy!
    Come this way, boy!
Who'll have a drink with me?
HENSLOWE. Why, here's a bird of wisdom sitting in the dark!
Shut your eyes, man, and use candles, or you'll scorch out your own
sockets! What's wrong now? But tell me that as we ride; for the
Queen wants you in a hurry, and what's more an angry Queen. I'd
not be you! Here I've hunted London for you from tavern to lady's
lodging till I ferreted out that Marlowe was here, and so I followed
him for news.

SHAKESPEARE. Here's news enough. Henslowe, look here!

HENSLOWE. Who did it?

SHAKESPEARE. We—he and I. There was another in it.

HENSLOWE. Was it the youngster passed me in the yard,
Caught at his horse and rode like fear away?

SHAKESPEARE. Was't a pale horse?

HENSLOWE. I saw not. In the dark
A voice cried "Hurry!"

SHAKESPEARE. That was she.

HENSLOWE. Who? Who?

SHAKESPEARE. Death. She has fled and left her catch behind.
Can you do anything?

HENSLOWE. For the living scarce—
You must be got away. Are you known here?

SHAKESPEARE. As men know Cain. All, all is finished,
Henslowe!

LANDLORD [*putting his head in at the door*]. Is anything wrong, sir?

HENSLOWE. Wrong? What should be wrong? But we're in haste. Call the ostler! We want a second horse.

> *He slips his arm through* SHAKESPEARE'S *and tries to lead him to the door.*

LANDLORD. Is the gentleman ill, sir? He sways.

HENSLOWE. Your good wine, host.

A MAN [*over the* LANDLORD'S *shoulder*]. The best on the Surrey side!

HENSLOWE. He'll tell the Queen so in an hour if you'll make way.

MEN [*crowding into the doorway*]. The Queen! Did you hear?
He's been sent by the Queen!

HENSLOWE. Keep your people back, landlord!

THE MAN [*staggering into the room*]. I say, three cheers for the Queen!

ANOTHER. The Queen! The Queen! Three cheers for Bess!

[*Singing*]. Hey, Bess! Ho, Bess!
Heel and toe, Bess!

Ladies and gentlemen, here's a man on the bed.

HENSLOWE. Ay! My friend! Let him be!

THE MAN. Is he drunk too?

THE OTHER. If I were a judge I'd say "Very drunk"! He's spilled his wine on his clothes. What I say is "Waste not, want not!"

LANDLORD. Come now, come away! You hear what the gentleman says.

THE MAN [*throwing him off*].

Hey, Death! Ho, Death!
Let me go, Death!

Shall I wake him?

SHAKESPEARE [*turning in the doorway*]. Ay, wake him, wake him, old trump of judgment! Wake him if you can,

And if you cannot let him sleep his sleep
And envy him that he can sleep so sound!

THE MAN. Ay sir, he shall sleep till he wakes. But we, sir, we'll sing you off the premises, for the love of Bess.

Hey, Bess! Ho, Bess!

ANOTHER [*hammering the table*]. Death, not Bess! Death! Death! Death! Come along chorus!

TWO OR THREE [*as they lurch out of the room*].

Ho, boy! Hey, boy!
Come this way, boy!
Who'll have a drink with me?

ALL [*following*].   Hey, Death! Ho, Death!
                          Out you go, Death!
                     We'll never drink with thee!

*The door swings to and quiet settles on the lightening room.
The first ray of sunlight touches the bed. Outside the birds
are beginning to sing.*

                    THE CURTAIN FALLS.

ACT IV.

A room in the palace, hung with tapestries. On the right wall is a heavy, studded door: on the left, a great raised seat on a low platform. On the back wall is a small curtained door and a large window. A girl in a primrose-coloured gown stands at it holding back its curtain. Set slantwise in front of it, nearer the centre of the stage, is a writing table with scattered papers. At it sits ELIZABETH, a secretary beside her. The Queen's dress is of dull grey brocade with transparent lawn and jewels of aquamarine; but as the evening deepens its colour becomes one with the dusk and only her white face and hands are clearly seen.

A HAWKER [*chanting in the street far away*].

> Cress! Buy cress!
> Who'll buy my cress-es?

ELIZABETH *lays down her pen.*

ELIZABETH. These three are signed. Take them to Walsingham. This I'll not grant. Tell him so! [*The man bows and goes out.*]

HAWKER [*nearer*].   Cress! Buy cress!

ELIZABETH. There! Put the papers by!

> *The girl at the window comes down to the table and begins to sort them.*

ANOTHER HAWKER.   Strawberries! Ripe strawberries!

THE GIRL.   I wonder, Madam, that you choose this room
Here on the noisy street.

ELIZABETH.   Child, when you marry
                    Who'll rule your nursery, you or your maids?

GIRL. Why, that I will!

ELIZABETH. Then you must sit in it daily. Where's Mary Fitton?

GIRL. In waiting, Madam, and half asleep. She was up early to-
day. I saw her from my window by the little garden door and called
to her. She had been out to pick roses, as you bade her, ere the
dew dried on them.

ELIZABETH. As I bade her?

GIRL. Yes, Madam, she said so.

HAWKER [*close at hand*].   Cress! Buy cress!
                    Fit for Queen Bess!

ELIZABETH. Open the window! [*The girl opens it.*]

HAWKER.   Cress! Buy cress!
                    Who'll buy my cress-es?

ELIZABETH. Fetch me my purse!

> *The girl goes out by the little door. As she does so,*
> ELIZABETH *takes her purse from a drawer and going to the*
> *window, throws out a coin.*

HAWKER.   Cress! Buy cress!
Are you there, lady? [ELIZABETH *throws out another coin.*]
                    I plucked my riches
                    From Deptford ditches,
                I came by a Deptford Inn;
                    Where a young man lies,
                    With pennies on his eyes—
Murdered, lady, and none saw who did it!
                    Cress! Buy cress!

> ELIZABETH *flings out another coin.*

There was a boy that ran away, and Henslowe the Queen's man, and
a third—   Cress! Buy cress!
                    A supper for Queen Bess!

> ELIZABETH *lays down the purse on the table as the girl comes back.*

GIRL [*distressed*]. Madam—

ELIZABETH. It was here. That cress seller has a sweet voice. Fling her a coin and ask her where she lives!

GIRL [*going to the window*]. Hey, beggar!

HAWKER. Bless you, lady!

GIRL. Where do you come from with your green stuff?

HAWKER. Marlow, lady, Marlow!

> Down by the river where the cresses grow,
> And buttercups like guineas.
> Cress! Buy cress!
> Who'll buy my cress-es?

Her voice dies away in the distance.

GIRL. She has come a long way.

> Marlow's across the river, far from us.

ELIZABETH. Marlowe's across the river, far from us. If any ask to speak with me, let me know it!

GIRL. Why, Madam, Henslowe, the old player, has been waiting since noon, and Mr. Shakespeare with him.

ELIZABETH. The name's not written here. Whose duty?

GIRL. Mary Fitton's.

ELIZABETH. Send Henslowe! And when I ring let Mary Fitton answer!

GIRL. I'll tell her, Madam.

> *She goes out. ELIZABETH rises and goes slowly across the room to the dais and seats herself. There is a pause. Then a page throws open the big door facing the dais and HENSLOWE enters.*

ELIZABETH.   Henslowe, you're not welcome
For the news you bring.

HENSLOWE.   Madam, that Marlowe's dead
I know because I found him—I am new come
    from Deptford—
But how you know I know not.

ELIZABETH.   Why, not a keel
Grounds on the Cornish pebbles, but the jar
Thrills through all English earth home to my
    feet.
No riderless horse snuffs blood and gallops home
To a girl widowed, but I the sparking hoofs
Hear pound as her heart pounds, waiting; for
    my spies
Are everywhere. Do not my English swifts
Report to me at dusk, eavesdropping low,
The number of my English primroses
In English woods all spring? The gulls on
    Thames
Scream past the Tower "Storm in Channel!
    Storm!"
And if I hear not, sudden my drinking glass
Rings out "Send help, lest English sailors
    drown!"
The lantern moon swings o'er unvisited towns
Signalling "Peace!" or a star shoots out of the
    west
Across my window, flashing "Danger here!"
And is it Ireland rising, or a child
On chalk-pit roof after the blackberries,
I'm warned, and bid my human servants haste.
The flat-worn stones, the echoes of the streets

> At night when drunkard's tumble, citizens
> In the half silence and half light trot home,
> Reveal the well, the ill in my own land.
> I am its eyes, its pulse, its finger-tips,
> The wakeful partner of its married soul.
> I know what darkness does, what dawn discovers
> In all the English country. I am the Queen.

You have done my errand? Shakespeare the player is with you?

HENSLOWE. He waits without.

ELIZABETH. Then he too was at Deptford last night.

HENSLOWE. None knows it.

ELIZABETH. That's well. But was it he, Henslowe—he?

HENSLOWE. No, no, no! I'll swear it.

ELIZABETH. But will he swear it?

HENSLOWE.   He's dazed, he will say anything—yes—no—
>   Just as you prompt him, as if one blow had
>   struck
>   His soul and Marlowe's body. Madam, he's not
>   his witness!
>   Yet, if 'twere true, if he has lost us Marlowe,
>   Must we lose him? Then has the English
>   stage
>   Lost both her hands and cannot feed herself,
>   Starves, Madam!

ELIZABETH.   You're honest, Henslowe! Your son's son one
>   day
>   May help a king to thread a needle's eye.
>   But do you think he did it?

HENSLOWE.   No, though he says it,
>   For he loved him.

ELIZABETH.   Loved him, but a woman better.

HENSLOWE. There was no woman with them.

ELIZABETH. So I hear; but a boy!

HENSLOWE. Unknown.

ELIZABETH. Did you see him?

HENSLOWE. Not his face. He was past me in a flash, crying "Hurry!"

ELIZABETH. Well, I'll see Shakespeare.

HENSLOWE. Madam—

ELIZABETH. I thread my own needles, Henslowe, being a woman. [MARY FITTON *enters.*] Send Mr. Shakespeare to me! [*Then, as* MARY *turns to go*—] Mary!

MARY. Madam?

ELIZABETH. Bid him hurry! [MARY *turns to the door.*] Mary!

MARY. Madam?

ELIZABETH. What did I tell you but now?

MARY. Madam, to bid him hurry.

HENSLOWE [*recognizing the voice*]. "Hurry!"

ELIZABETH. Wait. Daylight, Henslowe? Girl, you're slow. You go heavily. Have you not slept? Let Henslowe do your errand! [*To* HENSLOWE.] Let him wait at hand!

MARY. Madam, I can well go.

ELIZABETH. No hurry now. [HENSLOWE *goes out.*] D'you guess why I send for your teller of tales?

MARY. No, Madam.

ELIZABETH. He has told a tale, it seems, that I'd hear told again.

MARY. Told?

ELIZABETH. Why are you not in black, Mary?

MARY. I, Madam?

ELIZABETH. Marlowe is dead.

MARY. I grieve to hear it.

ELIZABETH. When did you hear?

MARY. Why, Madam, now—you tell me!

ELIZABETH. Then I tell you wrong. He is alive and has told all.

MARY. Alive?   They lie to you, Madam!   What has he told?
Who says it?

ELIZABETH.   You, Mary Fitton!   For by your dark-ringed
                     eyes
                  Your dreaming service and those blind hands of
                     yours
                  Seeking a hold, I think you saw him die,
                  Ere you passed Henslowe in the dark, crying
                     "Hurry!"

MARY.   Madam, it was your errand. For this Shakespeare,
                  This quill you thrust on me to sharpen up,
                  Jealous of Marlowe, though he had no cause
                  (What! must I live his nun, his stay-at-home?
                  Your servant and a lady of the court!),
                  Sent me a letter—

ELIZABETH.   Let me read!
MARY.   I tore it!
                  —so inked in threat that I post-haste for
                     Deptford—

ELIZABETH.   Ill judged!
MARY.   I know! I followed my first fear.
                  —rode to warn Marlowe. Shakespeare following,
                  Spying upon us, spying upon us, Madam!
                  Found us in counsel. Then, with a hail of words
                  That Marlowe would not bear, with "stale" and
                     "harlot,"
                  He beat me down, till Marlowe flung 'em back;
                  Then like two dogs they struggled. Marlowe fell.

ELIZABETH.   Struck down?
MARY.   Struck down, but blindly, not to kill—
                  I will not think to kill—and as he fell
                  His own knife caught him, here.

ELIZABETH.   What did you then?

MARY.   I, Madam?

ELIZABETH.   You, Madam? Did you fold your
                    hands
And watch this business as you'd watch a play,
And clap them on? Or, as a short month since
You played a part I think, did you strike in
And play a part? Why did you call for help?

MARY.   I did not, Madam!

ELIZABETH.   Why did not Mary Fitton
Cry help against—which lover?

MARY.   Lover, Madam?

ELIZABETH.   There's tinker, tailor, soldier—the old rhyme—
There's Pembroke, Marlowe, Shakespeare—

MARY.   Madam! Madam!
I'll not bear this!

ELIZABETH.   Ay, you have fierce black eyes—
What will you do then if you will not bear it?
You have leave to show.

MARY.   I say I did cry out
To both that they should cease.

ELIZABETH.   So you cried out!
Bring up your witnesses that heard you cry!

MARY.   I did not stand and watch. I ran upon them.
I was flung off and bruised.

ELIZABETH.   Show me the bruise!

MARY.   High on my arm—

ELIZABETH.   Rip up your sleeve and show me!
You stand, you stare, you're white. I think you
                    shake.

MARY.   Anger not fear, though you were ten times Queen
Of twenty Englands!

ELIZABETH.   Quiet, and quiet, my girl!
This ill-spent night has left you feverish.
You are too free for court,
Too bruised and touzled for my gentlemen.
You shall go home, I think, to heal this bruise,
To cleanse your body and soul in country air
And banished quiet till I send for you.

MARY.   Upon what count?

ELIZABETH.   On none. But I've no time,
No room for butter-fingers. Here's a man slain
Upon your lap that England needed. Go!
Go, blunted tool! [*She touches a bell.*]

MARY.   Madam! Madam! You wrong
                                                        me!

ELIZABETH.   I've wronged your betters, Mary, Mary Fitton,
As tide wrongs pebble, or as wind wrongs chaff
At threshing time.
                    A page enters at the great door on the right.
                                    Send Mr. Shakespeare to me!

MARY.   This is the justice of the Queen of England!

ELIZABETH.   My justice.

MARY.   Have I not served you?

ELIZABETH.   All things serve me.
They choose their path. I use them in their path.

MARY.   As once you used, they say—

ELIZABETH.   Do not dare! Do
                                                        not dare!

MARY.   Dare, Madam? May I not wonder, like another,
Why you have used me thus?

ELIZABETH.   I used you, dirt,
To show a man how foul the dirt can be;
But now I brush you from him.

The main door opens and HENSLOWE
enters followed by SHAKESPEARE.   *She*
beckons to HENSLOWE.

Henslowe!

HENSLOWE.   Madam?

They speak privately for a moment, then
HENSLOWE *goes out by the small door.*

MARY [*to* SHAKESPEARE].

You come to cue!

SHAKESPEARE.   What has fallen?

MARY.   Sent away

Because of you, because my name is Mary!

SHAKESPEARE.   Go to my lodging! Wait for me! I'll follow,
For where you go I go.

MARY.   Ay, bring your wife!

This act is over! There are other men!

She goes out.

SHAKESPEARE.   Mary! Love, life, the breath I breathe, come
back!

Mary, you have not heard me! Mary! Mary
Come back! [*The door shuts with a clang.*]

ANNE'S VOICE.   Come back!

ELIZABETH.   Never in any world!

Fasten the door there!

SHAKESPEARE [*struggling to open it*].   Open! Open, I say!

ELIZABETH.   Beat, beat your heart out! Let me watch you beat
Those servants of your soul until they bleed,
Mash, agonise, against a senseless door!
Beat, beat your weaker hands than that dead tree,
Tear, tear your nails upon its nails in vain.
Beat, beat your heart out—you'll not pass the
door!

Can you not come at her? She goes—beat, beat!
The distance widens, like a ship she goes
Utterly from you. Follow! Beat your hands!
What? Are you held, you who bow men with
    words
Windily down like corn-fields? Is she gone?
Call up the clouds to carry you who walk
Sky-high, star-level, eyeing the naked sun.
Where are your wings? Beat, beat your heart
    out! Beat!
Where is your strength? Will not the wood be
    moved?
Cannot your love-call reach her, you who know
The heart of the lark and how the warm throat
    thrills
At mating-time? Is there a living thing
You do not dwell in, cannot stir, and yet
You cannot move this door?

SHAKESPEARE.   I am not so bound—

ELIZABETH. Why, yes, there's the window! You may cast down and be done with it all—done with it all! I'll not stop you. Who am I to keep a man from his sweet rest? And yet—what of me, my son, before you do it? What of me and this England that I am?

SHAKESPEARE. Madam, I have not slept these five nights. I do not know what you say.

ELIZABETH. Or care?

SHAKESPEARE. Or care, Madam, forgive me! God's pity, Madam, open the door!

ELIZABETH. It shall not serve you.

SHAKESPEARE. I know it.

ELIZABETH. She has sold you, man.

SHAKESPEARE. I know it. Open the door!

ELIZABETH. Come here, my son! Why do I hold you here, think you?
SHAKESPEARE. Marlowe—
ELIZABETH. Tell me nothing! I'll know nothing! Mr. Shakespeare, where is the work I should have from you? Where is the new play? You sold and I bought. Give me my goods! Then go!

SHAKESPEARE. A play? You are Queen, Madam, you do not live our lives; so I call you not pure devilish to keep me here for so little a thing.

ELIZABETH.   Yet I will have it from you! There's paper, pen—
          I'll have your roughed-out scene ere Henslowe leaves
          To-night. And ere the ended month this play,
          This English laughter, ringing all her bells,
          Before the pick of Europe at my court
          Performed, shall link our hands with Italy,
          With old immortal Athens. This you'll do,
          For this you can.

SHAKESPEARE [crying out].   I am to live, not write,
          To love, not write of love, to live my life
          As others do; to live a summer life
          As all the others do!

ELIZABETH.   I thought so too
          When I was young. Then, 'mid my state affairs
          And droning voices of my ministers,
          The people's acclamation and the hiss
          Of treacheries to England and to me,
          Ever I heard the momentary clock
          Ticking away my girlhood as I reigned;
          While she—while she—
          Mary of Scotland, Mary of delight,
          (I know her sweetheart names) Maybird, May-flower,

The three times married honeysuckle queen,
She had her youth. Think you I'd not have
        changed,
Sat out her twenty years a prisoner,
Ridden her road from France to Fotheringay,
To have her story? Am I less woman, I,
That I'd not change with her? For the high way
Is flowerless, and thin the mountain air
And rends the lungs that breathe it; and the light
Spreading from hill to everlasting hill,
Welling across the sky as from a wound,
A heart of blood between the breasts of the
        world,
Is not much nearer, no, nor half as warm
As the kissing sun of the valleys: and we climb
(You'll climb as I do) not because we will,
Because we must. There is no virtue in it;
But some pride. Fate can force but not befool
        me!
I am not drunken with religious dream
Like the poor blissful fools of kingdom come:
I know the flesh is sweetest, when all's said,
And summer's heyday and the love of men:
I know well what I lose. I'm head of the Church
And stoop my neck on Sunday—to what Christ?
The God of little children? I have none.
The God of love? What love has come to me?
The God upon His ass? I am not meek,
Nor is he meek, the stallion that I ride,
The great white horse of England. I'll not bow
To the gentle Jesus of the women, I—
But to the man who hung 'twixt earth and heaven

Six mortal hours, and knew the end (as strength
And custom was) three days away, yet ruled
His soul and body so, that when the sponge
Blessed his cracked lips with promise of relief
And quick oblivion, he would not drink:
He turned his head away and would not drink:
Spat out the anodyne and would not drink.
This was a god for kings and queens of pride,
And him I follow.

SHAKESPEARE.   Whither?

ELIZABETH.   The alley's blind.
For the cross rules us or we rule the cross,
Yet the cross wins in the end.
For night is older than the daylight is:
The slack string will not quiver for the hand
Of cunningest musician.
Does the cross care, a chafer on a pin,
Whether Barabbas writhe, or very God?
All's one to the dead wood! Dead wood, dead
    wood,
It coffins us in the end. God, you and me
And everyone—the dead wood baffles all.
And why I care I know not, but I know
That I'll die fighting—and the fight goes on.
Yet not uncaptained shall the assault go on
Against dead wood fencing the hearts of men.
For this I chose you.
I am a barren woman. Mary's child
Reigns after me in England. Yet, to-night,
I crown my heir. I, England, crown my son.

SHAKESPEARE.   There was a better man but yesterday—
To him the crown! King was he of all song.

ELIZABETH.

He's king now of the silence after song,
When the last bell-note hovers, like a high
And starry rocket that dissolves in stars,
Lost ere they reach us. He is lord of that
For ever.

SHAKESPEARE.

He—he had the luck; but I,
But England was not lucky.

ELIZABETH.

Be assured
Had England chosen Marlowe, here to-night
England had crowned him, and you in Surrey
        ditch
Had lain where he lies, dead, my dead son, dead.
Take you the kingship on you!

SHAKESPEARE.
ELIZABETH.

A player-king—
As I a player-queen! I play my part
Not ill, not ill. Judge me, my English peer,
And witness for me, that I play not ill
My part! And if by night, unseen, I weep,
Scourging my spirit down the track of the years,
Hating the name of Mary, as she said;
Yet comes and goes my hour, and comes again,
My hour, when I bear England in my breast
As God Almighty bears His universe,
England moves in me, I for England speak,
As I speak now. It is not the shut door,
But I, but England, holds you prisoner.

SHAKESPEARE.
ELIZABETH.

But to what service, England, and what end?
I send my ships where never ships have sailed,
To break the barriers and make wide the ways
For the after world.

Send you your ships to the hidden lands of the
        soul,

To break the barriers and make plain the ways
Between man and man. Why else were we two
　　born?

SHAKESPEARE.　What's the worth of a play?
ELIZABETH.　　　　　　　　My ships are not so great
And ride not like firm islands of dry land
As Philip's do; yet these my cockle-boats
Have used the vast world as a village pound,
And fished for treasure above the planets' bed
In the drowned palaces where, water-bleached,
Atlantis gleams as gleams the skull-white moon,
Rolled in the overwhelming tides of time
Hither and down the beaches of the sky.
Send out your thoughts as I send out my men,
To earn a world for England!—paying first
The toll of the pioneer. I do not cheat.
Here is the bill—reckon it ere you pay!

SHAKESPEARE.　Have I not paid?
ELIZABETH.　　　　　　　Nay, hourly, till you die.
I tell you, you shall toss upon your bed
Crying "Let me sleep!" as men cry "Let me
　　live!"
And sleeping you shall still cry "Mary! Mary!"
This will not pass. Think not the sun that wakes
The birds in England and the daisy-lawns,
Draws up the meadow fog like prayer to heaven,
And curls the smoke in cottage chimney stacks,
Shall once forget to wake you with a warm
And kissing breath! The four walls shall repeat
The name upon your lips, and in your heart
The name, the one name, like a knife shall turn.
These are your dawns. *I* tell you, I who know.

Nor shall day spare you. All your prospering
    years,
The tasteless honours for yourself—not her—
The envy in men's voices, (if they knew
The beggar that they envied!) all this shall stab,
Stab, stab, and stab again. And little things
Shall hurt you so: stray words in books you read,
And jests of strangers never meant to hurt you:
The lovers in the shadow of your fence,
Their faces hid, shall thrust a spare hand out,
The other held, to stab you as you pass:
And oh, the cry of children when they play!
You shall put grief in irons and lock it up,
And at the door set laughter for a guard,
Yet dance through life on knives and never rest,
While England knows you for a lucky man.
These are your days. I tell you, I, a queen,
Ruling myself and half a world. I know
What fate is laid upon you. Carry it!
Or, if you choose, flinch, weaken, and fall down,
Lie flat and howl, and let the ones that love you
(Not burdened less) half carry it and you!
Will you do that? Proud man, will you do that?

SHAKESPEARE. Because you are all woman—

ELIZABETH.   Have you seen it?
None other sees.

SHAKESPEARE.   —and not as you're the Queen,
I'll let you be the tongue to my own soul,
Yet not for long I'll bear it.

ELIZABETH.   To each his angel
For good or ill.
Women to a man, the man to a woman ever

Mated or fated. I am this fate to you,
As to me once a fallen star you knew not.
It's long ago. You should have known the man.
He was the glory of the English night,
Its red star in decline. For see what came—
His fires were earthy and he choked himself
In his own ash. Not good but goodly was he,
A natural prince of the world: and he had been
        one
Had he been other, or I blind, or—Mary.
Lucifer! Lucifer! He loved me not,
But would have used me. Well—he used me
        not.
He died. I loved him. This between us two.
Bury it deep!

SHAKESPEARE.   Deep as my sorrow lies.
But Queen, what cometh after?

ELIZABETH.   Work.

SHAKESPEARE.   And after?

ELIZABETH.   Sleep comes for me.

SHAKESPEARE.   And after?

ELIZABETH.   Sleep for you.

SHAKESPEARE.   And after?

ELIZABETH.   Nothing. Only the blessed sleep.

SHAKESPEARE.   And so ends all?

ELIZABETH.   And so all ends.

SHAKESPEARE.   Love ends?

ELIZABETH.   And so love ends.

SHAKESPEARE.   I have a word to say.
Give me this crown and reach the sceptre here!
The end's not yet, but yet the end is mine;
For I know what I am and what I do

At last! Give me my pen, ere the spark dies
That lights me! And now leave me!

He turns to the table and his work.

ELIZABETH [*loudly*].   Open the door!
SHAKESPEARE.   Sesame, sesame! A word to say—

*The door is flung open and the long passage
is seen.*

O darkness, did she pass between your walls,
And left no picture on the empty air,
No echo of her step that waits for mine
To wake it in a message? What do I here?
"A word to say"! There's nothing left but words.

ELIZABETH *has descended from her throne
and crossing the room, pauses a moment
beside him.*

ELIZABETH.   Is the harness heavy—heavy?
SHAKESPEARE.   Heavy as lead.

Heavy as a heart.
ELIZABETH.   It will not lighten.
SHAKESPEARE.   Go! [*She goes out.*]

I had a word to say.
Oh, spark that burned but now—!
ANNE'S VOICE.   It dips, it dies—
SHAKESPEARE.   A night-light, fool, and not a star. I grope
Giddily in the dark. I shall grow old.
What is my sum? I have made seven plays,
Two poems and some sonnets. I have friends
So long as I write poems, sonnets, plays.
Earn then your loves, and as you like it—write!
Come, what's your will?

Three sets of lovers and a duke or two,
Courtiers and fool—We'll set it in a wood,
Half park, half orchard, like the woods at home.
See the house rustle, pit gape, boxes thrill,
As through the trees, boyishly, hand on hip,
Knee-deep in grass, zone-deep in margarets,
Comes to us—Mary!

ANNE'S VOICE.
                  Under the apple-trees,
In the spring, in the long grass—Will!

SHAKESPEARE.
                    Still the old shame
Hangs round my neck with withered arms and
    chokes
Endeavour.

ANNE'S VOICE.
           Will!

SHAKESPEARE.
              At right wing enter ghost!
It should be Marlowe with his parted mouth
And sweep of arm. Why should he wake for me?
That would be friendship, and what a friend was
    I!
Well—to the work!

ANNE'S VOICE.
           Will! Will!

SHAKESPEARE.
             What, ghost? still there?
Must I speak first? That's manners with the
    dead;
But this haunt lives—at Stratford, by the river.
Maggot, come out of my brain! Girl! Echo!
    Wraith!
You've had free lodging, like a rat, too long.
I need my room. Come, show yourself and go!
"Changed?" "But I knew her!"—Say your
    say and go!
You'd a tongue once.

ANNE'S VOICE.   You're to be great—

SHAKESPEARE.   Stale! Stale!
That's the Queen's catch-word.

ANNE'S VOICE.   But I know, I know,
I'm your poor village woman, but I know
What you must learn and learn, and shriek to
    God
To spare you learning—

SHAKESPEARE.   Ay, like wheels that shriek,
Carting the grain, their dragged unwilling way
Over the stones, uphill, at even, thus,
Shrieking, I learn—

ANNE'S VOICE.   When harvest comes—

SHAKESPEARE.   Is come!
Sown, sprouted, scythed and garnered—

ANNE'S VOICE.   I alone
Can give you comfort, for you reap my pain,
As I your loss—loss—loss—

SHAKESPEARE.   Anne, was it thus?

ANNE'S VOICE.   No other way—

SHAKESPEARE.   Such pain?

ANNE'S VOICE.   Such pain, such pain!

SHAKESPEARE.   I did not know. O tortured thing, remember,
I did not know—I did not know! Forgive—

ANNE'S VOICE.   Forgiving is forgetting—no, come back!
I love you. Oh, come back to me, come back!

SHAKESPEARE.   I cannot.

ANNE'S VOICE.   Oh, come back! I love you so.

SHAKESPEARE.   Be still, poor voice, be still!

ANNE'S VOICE.   I love you so.

SHAKESPEARE.   What is this love?
What is this awful spirit and unknown.

That mates the suns and gives a bird his tune?
What is this stirring at the roots of the world?
What is this secret child that leaps in the womb
Of life? What is this wind, whence does it blow,
And why? And falls upon us like the flame
Of Pentecost, haphazard. What is this dire
And holy ghost that will not let us two
For no prayers' sake nor good deeds' sake nor
    pain
Nor pity, have peace, and live at ease, and die
As the leaves die?

ANNE'S VOICE.   I know not. All I know,
Is that I love you.

SHAKESPEARE.   But I know, having learned—
This I believe because I know, I know,
Being in hell, paying the price, alone,
Licked in the flame unspeakable and torn
By devils, as in the old tales that are true—
All true, the fires, the red hot branding irons,
The thirst, the laughter, and the filth of shame,
All true, O fellow men! all true, all true—
Down through the circles, like a mangled rat
A hawk lets fall from the far towers of the sky,
Down through the wakeful æons of the night,
Into the Pit of misery they call
Bottomless, falling—I believe and know
That the Pit's bottom is the lap of God,
And God is love.

ANNE'S VOICE.   Is love, is love—

SHAKESPEARE.   I know.
And knowing I will live my dark days out
And wait for His own evening to give light.

And though I may not fill the mouth I love,
Yet will I sow and reap and bind my sheaves,
Glean, garner, mill my corn, and bake, and cast
My bread upon the waters of the age.
This will I do for love's sake, lest God's eyes,
That are the Judgment, ask her man of her
One day, and she be shamed—as I am shamed
Ever, in my heart, by a voice witnessing
Against me that I knew not love.

PAGE [*entering with lights*].   The Queen, sir,
Has sent you candles, now the sun is down,
That you may see to work.

SHAKESPEARE.   I thank the Queen.
Tell her the work goes well!

      He sits down at the table.

                     Act one, scene one,
Oliver's house. It *shall* go well. I have
A strength that comes I know not whence. It
    shall
Go well. And then I'll give the Roman tale
I heard at school—a tale of men, not women:
That easies all. But Antony goes on
To Egypt and a gipsy: leaves his pale wife
At home to scald her eyes out. Mary—Mary—
Will you not let me be? It *shall* go well.
And after Antony some Twelfth Night trick
To please our gods and give my pregnancy
Its needed peace. How many months for Den-
    mark?
And then? A whole man laughs, and so will I.
Oh, Smile behind the thunder, teach me laughter,

And save my soul!—
The knock-about fat man, try him again!
He'll take a month or less—candles are cheap,
Cheaper than sleep these dreaming nights. That
    done,
I'll sink another shaft in Holinshed—
Marlowe, your diamonds! your diamonds!
The king and his three daughters—he's been
    shaped
Already. True! But rough cut only. Wait!
Give me that giant cluster in my hand
To cut anew, in its own midnight set,
It shall outshine Orion! Afterwards,
A fairy tale maybe, and after that—
And after that—and after—after? God!
The years before me! And no Mary! Mary—

ANNE'S VOICE.   When her lost face—

SHAKESPEARE.   It shall, it shall go well.

ANNE'S VOICE.   —stares from the page you toil upon, thus, thus,
In a glass of tears—

SHAKESPEARE.   They scald, they blind my view,
No comfort anywhere.

ANNE'S VOICE.   I love you so.

SHAKESPEARE.   The work, the work remains.

ANNE'S VOICE.   But when you're old,
For work too old, or pity, love or hate,
For anything but peace, and in your hand
Lies the crowned life victorious at last—

SHAKESPEARE.   Like the crowned Indian fruit, the voyage home
Rots while it gilds, not worth the tasting—

ANNE'S VOICE.   Then,
Remember me! Then, then, when all your need

Is hands to serve you and a breast to die on,
Come back to me!

SHAKESPEARE.   God knows—some day?
ANNE'S VOICE.   I wait.

As he stoops over his work again

THE CURTAIN FALLS

January, 1920—April, 1921.